THE YEAR OF THE
BLACKHAWKS

2010
STANLEY CUP
CHAMPIONS

Fenn Publishing Company Ltd.

The Year of the Blackhawks:
Celebrating Chicago's 2009-10 Stanley Cup Championship Season
A Fenn Publishing Book / First Published in 2010

The publisher gratefully acknowledges the support of the Canada Council
for the Arts and the Ontario Arts Council for its publishing program.
We acknowledge the support of the Government of Ontario through the
Ontario Media Development Corporation's Ontario Book Initiative.

THE CANADA COUNCIL | LE CONSEIL DES ARTS
FOR THE ARTS | DU CANADA
SINCE 1957 | DEPUIS 1957

ONTARIO ARTS COUNCIL
CONSEIL DES ARTS DE L'ONTARIO

We acknowledge the financial support of the Government of Canada through the Book
Publishing Industry Development Program (BPIDP) for our publishing activities.

Care has been taken to trace ownership of copyright material in this book and to secure
permissions. The publisher will gladly receive any information that will enable them
to rectify errors or omissions.

Designed by First Image
Fenn Publishing Company Ltd.
Toronto, Ontario, Canada
Printed in Canada

All photographs copyright NHL/Getty Images.

Library and Archives Canada Cataloguing in Publication data available upon request

Mixed Sources
Cert no. SW-COC-001271
© 1996 FSC
FSC

The OFFICIAL NHL Stanley Cup Publication

THE YEAR OF THE
BLACKHAWKS

Celebrating Chicago's 2009-10 Stanley Cup Championship Season

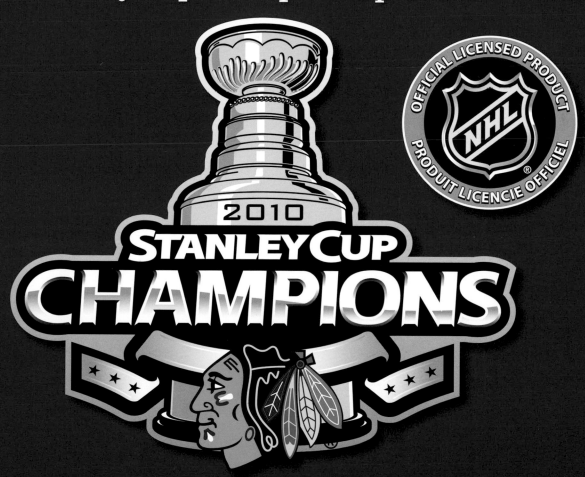

Andrew Podnieks

Fenn Publishing Company Ltd.
Toronto, Canada

CONTENTS

Stanley Cup Final

Chicago wins Stanley Cup 4-2

Team History

The longest season in the storied history of the Chicago Blackhawks has ended with the team's greatest Stanley Cup triumph. Some 110 games and 264 days after playing their first exhibition game, the Hawks beat Philadelphia in a thrilling Final for the team's first Cup win in 49 years.

Any team that wins the Cup doesn't win it on the first day of training camp or the last day of the season. Rather, it's a process. The Hawks started on September 19, losing a 3-2 overtime decision to Washington, the first of four pre-season games in North America before embarking on an ambitious tour of Europe.

That tour included an exhibition game against Davos, a Swiss team, followed by a game against Zurich for the Victoria Cup. From there, the Hawks traveled to Helsinki for a pair of regular-season games against the Florida Panthers to kick off the 2009-10 season.

The team then returned to North America to play the rest of the 82-game schedule, and that, too, was a process. Coach Joel Quenneville wasn't sure how his goaltending was going to work out, for instance. Cristobal Huet signed a big contract in the off season, so he seemed to be the number-one man. But over the course of the year, backup Antti Niemi played an ever-greater role in the team's fortunes, and in the end it was the Finn who supplanted the Frenchman as the go-to goalie.

Up front, the team was led by captain Jonathan Toews and Patrick Kane. The pair was young, skilled, and friends off ice, and the Hawks relied on these two to get the team's offense in gear. Midway through the season, they were opponents for a couple of important weeks when the league shut down to allow its players to participate in the 2010 Olympic Winter Games in Vancouver. And there, front and centre, was Toews with Team Canada and Kane with Team USA.

In the end, Chicago finished second overall in the Western Conference with 112 points, one behind San Jose, but this meant little once the game's "second season" started and every team had to prove itself all over again.

The Hawks faced adversity right away in the first two rounds, losing the opening game on home ice each time. But for their worrisome opening games, they played spectacularly on the road, winning seven in a row at one stretch to tie an NHL record. Against Nashville, they were tentative in the first game but quickly found their footing. Then, they were unable to close out the Canucks on home ice in Game Five of the Conference semi-final, but they bounced right back and won two nights later in Vancouver.

They followed this with a remarkably impressive sweep of San Jose to advance to the Stanley Cup Final, and their performance in the ultimate series was nothing short of sensational.

Although Toews and Kane were important to the team, the Hawks had so many heroes on so many nights. Big Dustin Byfuglien was sensational. Dave Bolland did so many things needed for victory. Marian Hossa scored huge goals. It was truly a team victory.

The Hawks also dispelled two myths. They went all the way despite starting the season off in Europe (as Pittsburgh had done in 2008-09, in fact), and they proved that a team with many Olympians could use that grand event as a final spark for a playoff run.

Most important, the Hawks won playing an offense-first game. No centre-ice trap. No obstruction. Just speed and skill and goals and thrills. Their victory promises a great future for the team and the game.

The Chicago Blackhawks were one of three American teams to join the NHL for the 1926-27 season, along with the Detroit Cougars (later Red Wings) and New York Rangers. The Hawks were owned by Frederic McLaughlin, who had made his fortune in the coffee business, and was a veteran of the First World War with a unit nicknamed the Blackhawk Division. McLaughlin's wife, Irene Castle, designed the team logo, and although it has undergone many subtle changes over the years, the Indian head has been consistent from the first day.

For most of his time with the team, McLaughlin was both owner and general manager. The Blackhawks played their first game on November 17, 1926, at the Chicago Coliseum, beating the Toronto St. Pats (later Maple Leafs) by a 4-1 score. It wasn't until early in the 1929-30 season that the team moved into the much larger Chicago Stadium, its home for the next 65 years. The Stadium was famous for its huge and loud pipe organ, the only one of its kind in an NHL arena and the mechanism that became world-famous for encouraging fans to cheer on their team.

Although not an instant success, the Hawks soon became a very good hockey team, making the Stanley Cup Final in 1931 and winning the Cup twice in the 1930s, first in '34 and again in '38. McLaughlin believed American players could compete with Canadian, and the 1938 team was mostly U.S.-born. Although that season was successful, the experiment soon proved disastrous and McLaughlin abandoned the strategy.

McLaughlin passed away in 1944, and for most of the next 15 years the Hawks were among the worst teams in the NHL. Their fortunes changed when they signed three future greats—Bobby Hull, Stan Mikita, and Pierre Pilote—and acquired Glenn Hall from the Red Wings. The team quickly joined the elite, and in 1961 it won the third Stanley Cup in franchise history. They reached the Final again in 1962 and 1965, but lost to Toronto and Montreal, respectively.

The Hawks missed the playoffs in 1968-69, but then began one of the longest runs of success in professional sports, making the playoffs in 28 consecutive seasons. While Mikita and Hull were now in the twilight of their careers, a new generation of stars was on the rise, notably goaltender Tony Esposito and Bobby's younger brother, Dennis. They made it all the way to the Final in 1971 and '73, losing to Montreal on both occasions, and didn't make it back until 1992.

The Hawks played their final game at the Stadium on April 28, 1994, a 1-0 loss to Toronto. They moved into the modern United Center to start the 1994-95 season and have been there ever since.

The Hawks had a difficult time between 1997 and 2008, making the playoffs only once in ten seasons. They were rejuvenated in 2007 when Rocky Wirtz took over as team owner after his father Bill passed away. Rocky instilled a renewed energy in the team and reconnected with the fans.

Goalie Chuck Gardiner joined the Blackhawks in their second season, 1927-28, and played with the team for seven seasons. He played every game for the last six years and was the only goalie to captain a team to the Stanley Cup, which he did in 1934. He died at age 29 because of a brain hemorrhage and was a charter member of the Hockey Hall of Fame in 1945.

The Stadium

The Hawks played their first game at the Chicago Stadium on December 15, 1929, a 3-1 win over the Pittsburgh Pirates before a team-record crowd of 14,212. Nicknamed the "Madhouse on Madison," it last hosted an NHL game on April 28, 1994, when the Toronto Maple Leafs beat Chicago 1-0 in a playoff game.

The United Center

Home to the Blackhawks since 1994-95, the United Center is the largest arena in the United States. Although the official capacity is listed as 17,717, it has frequently held more than 22,000 as the team has rocketed to the top of the attendance standings in the NHL.

Player	2009-10 Status	Player	2009-10 Status
Akim Aliu	Rockford IceHogs	Adam Hobson	Rockford IceHogs/Toledo
Cam Barker	Blackhawks/Minnesota	Justin Hodgman	traded to Toronto
Kyle Beach	Rockford IceHogs	Marian Hossa	Blackhawks
Dan Bertram	DNP	Cristobal Huet	Blackhawks
Bryan Bickell	Blackhawks/Rockford IceHogs	Aaron Johnson	traded to Calgary
Dave Bolland	Blackhawks	Patrick Kane	Blackhawks
Daryl Boyle	Rockford IceHogs	Bracken Kearns	Rockford IceHogs
Michael Brennan	Rockford IceHogs	Duncan Keith	Blackhawks
Evan Brophey	Rockford IceHogs	Matt Keith	Rockford IceHogs
Troy Brouwer	Blackhawks	Rob Klinkhammer	Rockford IceHogs
Adam Burish	Blackhawks	Tomas Kopecky	Blackhawks
Dustin Byfuglien	Blackhawks	Andrew Ladd	Blackhawks
Brian Campbell	Blackhawks	Shawn Lalonde	Rockford IceHogs
Jonathan Carlsson	Rockford IceHogs/Toledo	Peter MacArthur	Rockford IceHogs
Joe Charlebois	Rockford IceHogs/Toledo	John Madden	Blackhawks
Brian Connelly	Rockford IceHogs	Derek Nesbitt	Rockford IceHogs/Toledo
Corey Crawford	Rockford IceHogs	Antti Niemi	Blackhawks
Mark Cullen	Rockford IceHogs	Joe Palmer	played in CHL
Simon Danis-Pepin	Rockford IceHogs	David Phillips	Rockford IceHogs/Toledo
Nathan Davis	Rockford IceHogs	Alec Richards	Rockford IceHogs/Toledo
Jake Dowell	Rockford IceHogs	Jean-Claude Sawyer	Rockford IceHogs/Toledo
Ben Eager	Blackhawks	Brent Seabrook	Blackhawks
Bryan Ewing	Rockford IceHogs/Springfield	Patrick Sharp	Blackhawks
Joe Fallon	Rockford IceHogs/Peoria	Jack Skille	Rockford IceHogs
Colin Fraser	Blackhawks	Radek Smolenak	Blackhawks/AHL
Byron Froese	returned to WHL	Brent Sopel	Blackhawks
David Gilbert	returned to QMJHL	Maxime Tanguay	Rockford IceHogs/Toledo
Jordan Hendry	Blackhawks	Jonathan Toews	Blackhawks
Niklas Hjalmarsson	Blackhawks	Kris Versteeg	Blackhawks
Adam Hobson	Rockford IceHogs/Toledo	Teigan Zahn	returned to WHL

Danny Bois of the Blackhawks is hounded by Washington's ace Alexander Ovechkin during a pre-season game on September 23, 2009.

Coach Joel Quenneville
b. Windsor, Ontario, September 15, 1958

A life in hockey—first as a player and now as a coach—has taken Joel Quenneville from the 1970s to the 21st century. It has also given him his first Stanley Cup as a head coach.

Drafted by the Toronto Maple Leafs in 1978, Quenneville played in the NHL for 13 years with five teams. He was known as a big, strong, stay-at-home defenceman, but he never had a chance to raise the Cup. Quenneville's last season as a player was also his first as a coach. In 1991-92, he was a playing coach with the St. John's Maple Leafs, Toronto's AHL affiliate, and soon after he was named head coach of the Springfield Indians.

Quenneville served as an assistant coach in Quebec and later Colorado during the team's move from Canada to Denver, helping the team to victory in the 1996 Stanley Cup Final.

That same year, Quenneville was hired by the St. Louis Blues as head coach, and over the next eight seasons he became the most successful coach in team history, compiling a record of 307-191-95. The team made the playoffs every full season he was in St. Louis, and in 1999-2000 he was named winner of the Jack Adams Trophy.

In 2004, he was named head coach of the Avs. Just four games into the 2008-09 season, he became coach of the Blackhawks, immediately turning the young team into an offensive, exciting juggernaut. The Hawks went to the Conference Final in 2009, and a year later they won it all.

Joel Quenneville calmly watches the game from behind the bench.

SEPTEMBER 29, 2009
HALLENSTADION—ZURICH, SWITZERLAND
ZURICH LIONS 2-CHICAGO BLACKHAWKS 1

Backed by superb goaltending form their 40-year-old starter, the Zurich Lions beat the NHL's Blackhawks by a 2-1 score to reclaim the Victoria Cup. In 2008, the New York Rangers claimed the inaugural edition of the NHL vs. Europe's best with a 4-3 win over Metallurg Magnitogorsk.

The Lions were not intimidated by Chicago's 9-2 pasting of HC Davos in the exhibition tuneup to this Victoria Cup, but the Hawks had control of the game early on. Cam Barker's one-timer slipped under the arm of Sulander to give the visitors the early lead, but it was to be the only goal they'd score this night.

Zurich tied the game six minutes later on a great pass by Thibaut Monnet to spring Patrick Bartschi in alone on goalie Antti Niemi. Bartschi made a great move and roofed a backhand over the sprawling goalie to tie the score and send the home crowd into a frenzy of excitement.

Lukas Grauwiler got the game winner in the middle period when he scooped in a loose puck after Niemi failed to control a shot from Cyrill Buhler.

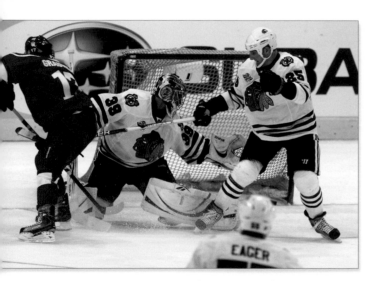

Lukas Grauwiler of Zurich scores the game-winning goal against Cristobal Huet during the 2009 Victoria Cup in Switzerland.

Victoria Cup Game

Lineups

Zurich—GK: Ari Sulander, Lukas Flueler (DNP)—Defence: Radoslav Suchy, Philippe Schelling, Mathias Seger, Daniel Schnyder, Patrick Geering, Andre Signoretti, Andri Stoffel—Forwards: Domenico Pittis, Peter Sejna, Mark Bastl, Jean-Guy Trudel, Jan Alston, Ryan Gardner, Thibaut Monnet, Patrick Bartschi, Blaine Down, Cyrill Buhler, Lukas Grauwiler, Oliver Kamber

Chicago—GK: Cristobal Huet, Antti Niemi (DNP)—Defence: Duncan Keith, Brent Seabrook, Niklas Hjalmarsson, Brian Campbell, Brent Sopel, Cam Barker—Forwards: Jonathan Toews, Troy Brouwer, Patrick Kane, Patrick Sharp, Andrew Ladd, Dave Bolland, Dustin Byfuglien, Ben Eager, Tomas Kopecky, Jack Skille, Kris Versteeg, Colin Fraser, Radek Smolenak

Game Summary

FIRST PERIOD
0-1   Chicago, Barker (Sharp) 6:13
1-1   Zurich, Bartschi (Monnet, Signoretti) 12:25
Penalties: Pittis (ZSC, 2:53), Pittis (ZSC, 14:11), Sharp (CHI, 15:17)

SECOND PERIOD
2-1   Zurich, Grauwiler (Buhler) 14:44
Penalties: Down (ZSC, 7:59), Seger (ZSC, 9:34) & Byfuglien (CHI, 9:34), Trudel (ZSC, 17:32)

THIRD PERIOD
No Scoring
Penalties: Monnet (ZSC, 8:28), Byfuglien (CHI, 9:43), Skille (CHI, 13:16), Bastl (ZSC, 14:04), Bolland (CHI, 14:19)
Missed Penalty Shot: Bartschi (ZSC, 16:46)

IN GOAL
ZSC—Sulander
CHI—Huet

SHOTS ON GOAL

ZSC	7	6	9	22
CHI	11	12	12	35

Referees—Dan Marouelli (CAN)
        Vyacheslav Bulanov (RUS)
Linesmen—Tim Nowak (USA)
        Frantisek
        Kalivoda (CZE)

Attendance: 9,744

Kamil Kreps skates away from Niklas Hjalmarsson (#4) during the second of two games Chicago and Florida played in Helsinki to begin the 2009-10 NHL season. Finnish goalie Antti Niemi recorded the shutout in a 4-0 Blackhawks win. One night earlier, the Panthers were the victors, 4-3 in a shootout.

EASTERN CONFERENCE

Northeast Division

	GP	W	L	OT	GF	GA	Pts
Buffalo	82	45	27	10	235	207	100
Ottawa	82	44	32	6	225	238	94
Boston	82	39	30	13	206	200	91
Montreal	82	39	33	10	217	223	88
Toronto	82	30	38	14	214	267	74

Southeast Division

	GP	W	L	OT	GF	GA	Pts
Washington	82	54	15	13	318	233	121
Atlanta	82	35	34	13	234	256	83
Carolina	82	35	37	10	230	256	80
Tampa Bay	82	34	36	12	217	260	80
Florida	82	32	37	13	208	244	77

Atlantic Division

	GP	W	L	OT	GF	GA	Pts
New Jersey	82	48	27	7	222	191	103
Pittsburgh	82	47	28	7	257	237	101
Philadelphia	82	41	35	6	236	225	88
NY Rangers	82	38	33	11	222	218	87
NY Islanders	82	34	37	11	222	264	79

WESTERN CONFERENCE

Central Division

	GP	W	L	OT	GF	GA	Pts
Chicago	82	52	22	8	271	209	112
Detroit	82	44	24	14	229	216	102
Nashville	82	47	29	6	225	225	100
St. Louis	82	40	32	10	225	223	90
Columbus	82	32	35	15	216	259	79

Northwest Division

	GP	W	L	OT	GF	GA	Pts
Vancouver	82	49	28	5	272	222	103
Colorado	82	43	30	9	244	233	95
Calgary	82	40	32	10	204	210	90
Minnesota	82	38	36	8	219	246	84
Edmonton	82	27	47	8	214	284	62

Pacific Division

	GP	W	L	OT	GF	GA	Pts
San Jose	82	51	20	11	264	215	113
Phoenix	82	50	25	7	225	202	107
Los Angeles	82	46	27	9	241	219	101
Anaheim	82	39	32	11	238	251	89
Dallas	82	37	31	14	237	254	88

REGULAR SEASON RESULTS, 2009-10

~all shutouts are recorded in square brackets; all overtime scorers are listed; all scorers in 1-0 games are listed; all shootout games are noted

October 2	Florida 4 at Chicago 3 (SO) (played in Helsinki)
October 3	Chicago 4 at Florida 0 [Niemi] (played in Helsinki)
October 8	Chicago 2 at Detroit 3
October 10	Colorado 3 at Chicago 4 (SO)
October 12	Calgary 5 at Chicago 6 (Seabrook 0:26 OT)
October 14	Edmonton 3 at Chicago 4
October 15	Chicago 3 at Nashville 1
October 17	Dallas 4 at Chicago 3
October 21	Vancouver 3 at Chicago 2
October 24	Nashville 0 at Chicago 2 [Huet]
October 26	Minnesota 1 at Chicago 3
October 29	Chicago 0 at Nashville 2 [Rinne]
October 30	Montreal 2 at Chicago 3
November 5	Chicago 1 at Phoenix 3
November 6	Chicago 3 at Colorado 4 (SO)
November 9	Los Angeles 1 at Chicago 4
November 11	Colorado 2 at Chicago 3 (SO)
November 13	Toronto 2 at Chicago 3
November 15	San Jose 3 at Chicago 4 (Seabrook 0:41 OT)
November 19	Chicago 7 at Calgary 1
November 21	Chicago 5 at Edmonton 2
November 22	Chicago 1 at Vancouver 0 (Bickell 1:12 3rd) [Niemi]
November 25	Chicago 7 at San Jose 2
November 27	Chicago 0 at Anaheim 3 [Giguere]
November 28	Chicago 1 at Los Angeles 2 (SO)
December 1	Columbus 3 at Chicago 4 (SO)
December 4	Nashville 4 at Chicago 1
December 5	Chicago 2 at Pittsburgh 1 (Versteeg 2:38 OT)
December 9	NY Rangers 1 at Chicago 2 (Byfuglien 3:43 OT)
December 11	Chicago 1 at Buffalo 2
December 13	Tampa Bay 0 at Chicago 4 [Niemi]
December 16	St. Louis 0 at Chicago 3 [Huet]
December 18	Boston 4 at Chicago 5 (SO)
December 20	Detroit 0 at Chicago 3 [Huet]
December 22	San Jose 3 at Chicago 2
December 23	Chicago 3 at Detroit 0 [Niemi]
December 26	Chicago 4 at Nashville 1
December 27	Nashville 4 at Chicago 5
December 29	Chicago 4 at Dallas 5
December 31	New Jersey 1 at Chicago 5
January 2	Chicago 6 at St. Louis 3
January 3	Anaheim 2 at Chicago 5
January 5	Minnesota 1 at Chicago 4
January 7	Chicago 5 at Boston 2
January 9	Chicago 5 at Minnesota 6 (SO)
January 10	Anaheim 3 at Chicago 1
January 14	Columbus 0 at Chicago 3 [Huet]
January 16	Chicago 6 at Columbus 5
January 17	Chicago 4 at Detroit 3 (SO)
January 19	Chicago 1 at Ottawa 4
January 21	Chicago 3 at Calgary 1
January 23	Chicago 1 at Vancouver 5
January 26	Chicago 4 at Edmonton 2
January 28	Chicago 4 at San Jose 3 (Brouwer 1:37 OT)
January 30	Chicago 2 at Carolina 4
February 3	St. Louis 3 at Chicago 2
February 5	Phoenix 2 at Chicago 1 (SO)
February 6	Chicago 2 at St. Louis 1
February 9	Dallas 3 at Chicago 4 (SO)
February 13	Atlanta 4 at Chicago 5 (SO)
February 14	Chicago 5 at Columbus 4 (SO)

OLYMPICS BREAK

March 2	Chicago 3 at NY Islanders 5
March 3	Edmonton 2 at Chicago 5
March 5	Vancouver 3 at Chicago 6
March 7	Detroit 5 at Chicago 4
March 10	Los Angeles 2 at Chicago 3 (Sharp 2:08 OT)
March 13	Chicago 2 at Philadelphia 3
March 14	Washington 4 at Chicago 3 (Backstrom 3:10 OT)
March 17	Chicago 2 at Anaheim 4
March 18	Chicago 3 at Los Angeles 0 [Niemi]
March 20	Chicago 4 at Phoenix 5 (SO)
March 23	Phoenix 0 at Chicago 2 [Niemi]
March 25	Chicago 3 at Columbus 8
March 28	Columbus 4 at Chicago 2
March 30	Chicago 2 at St. Louis 4
March 31	Chicago 4 at Minnesota 0 [Niemi]
April 2	Chicago 2 at New Jersey 1 (SO)
April 4	Calgary 1 at Chicago 4
April 6	Chicago 5 at Dallas 2
April 7	St. Louis 5 at Chicago 6
April 9	Chicago 5 at Colorado 2
April 11	Detroit 3 at Chicago 2 (Stuart 3:11 OT)

Chicago's captain Jonathan Toews celebrates Olympic gold with Canada in Vancouver.

Patrick Kane of Team USA is hounded by Sidney Crosby but maintains control of the puck in the gold-medal game.

Six members of Chicago's 2009-10 team played at the 2010 Olympics, and four were involved in the historic gold-medal game the afternoon of February 28, 2010. Canada defeated the United States 3-2 in overtime to win gold. The United States won silver. Slovakia, meanwhile, lost the bronze-medal game to Finland, 5-3.

Chicago captain Jonathan Toews was named the Best Forward by the IIHF Directorate. He tied for third in scoring and was also named by the media to the All-Star team.

Chicago's captain Jonathan Toews and Patrick Kane (left) enjoy a video tribute for their Olympic participation during the Hawks' first home game after Vancouver 2010.

CANADA—GOLD

	GP	G	A	P	Pim
Jonathan Toews	7	1	7	8	2
Duncan Keith	7	0	6	6	2
Brent Seabrook	7	0	1	1	2

USA—SILVER

	GP	G	A	P	Pim
Patrick Kane	6	3	2	5	2

SLOVAKIA—FOURTH

	GP	G	A	P	Pim
Marian Hossa	7	3	6	9	6
Tomas Kopecky	7	1	0	1	2

Chicago's Olympians of 2010 (l to r)—Tomas Kopecky, Marian Hossa, Patrick Kane, Jonathan Toews, Duncan Keith, Brent Seabrook.

Skaters	Team(s)	GP	G	A	P	Pim
Barker, Cam	CHI/MIN	70	5	16	21	68
Bickell, Bryan	CHI	16	3	1	4	5
Bolland, Dave	CHI	39	6	10	16	28
Boynton, Nick	ANA/CHI	49	1	7	8	71
Brouwer, Troy	CHI	78	22	18	40	66
Burish, Adam	CHI	13	1	3	4	14
Byfuglien, Dustin	CHI	82	17	17	34	94
Campbell, Brian	CHI	68	7	31	38	18
Dowell, Jake	CHI	3	1	1	2	5
Eager, Ben	CHI	60	7	9	16	120
Ebbett, Andrew	ANA/CHI/MIN	61	9	6	15	8
Fraser, Colin	CHI	70	7	12	19	44
Hendry, Jordan	CHI	43	2	6	8	10
Hjalmarsson, Niklas	CHI	77	2	15	17	20
Hossa, Marian	CHI	57	24	27	51	18
Johnsson, Kim	MIN/CHI	60	7	10	17	30
Kane, Patrick	CHI	82	30	58	88	20
Keith, Duncan	CHI	82	14	55	69	51
Kopecky, Tomas	CHI	74	10	11	21	28
Ladd, Andrew	CHI	82	17	21	38	67
Madden, John	CHI	79	10	13	23	12
Seabrook, Brent	CHI	78	4	26	30	59
Sharp, Patrick	CHI	82	25	41	66	28
Skille, Jack	CHI	6	1	1	2	0
Smolenak, Radek	CHI	1	0	0	0	5
Sopel, Brent	CHI	73	1	7	8	34
Toews, Jonathan	CHI	76	25	43	68	47
Versteeg, Kris	CHI	79	20	24	44	35

Goalies	Team(s)	GP	W-L-OTL	Mins	GA	SO	GAA
Crawford, Corey	CHI	1	0-1-0	59	3	0	3.05
Huet, Cristobal	CHI	48	26-14-4	2,731	114	4	2.50
Niemi, Antti	CHI	39	26-7-4	2,190	82	7	2.25

Roster Moves

Andrew Ebbett claimed off waivers by Chicago from Anaheim on October 17, 2009; claimed off waivers by Minnesota from Chicago on November 21, 2009

Cam Barker traded by Chicago to Minnesota on February 12, 2010, for Kim Johnsson and Nick Leddy

Nick Boynton traded by Anaheim to Chicago on March 2, 2010, for future considerations

St. Louis forward David Backes tries to score, but is thwarted by goalie Antti Niemi and defenceman Brent Seabrook.

EASTERN CONFERENCE QUARTER-FINAL

Montreal (8) vs. Washington (1)

April 15	Montreal 3 at Washington 2 (Plekanec 13:19 OT)
April 17	Montreal 5 at Washington 6 (Backstrom 0:31 OT)
April 19	Washington 5 at Montreal 1
April 21	Washington 6 at Montreal 3
April 23	Montreal 2 at Washington 1
April 26	Washington 1 at Montreal 4
April 28	Montreal 2 at Washington 1

Washington wins best-of-seven 4-3

Philadelphia (7) vs. New Jersey (2)

April 14	Philadelphia 2 at New Jersey 1
April 16	Philadelphia 3 at New Jersey 5
April 18	New Jersey 2 at Philadelphia 3 (Carcillo 3:35 OT)
April 20	New Jersey 1 at Philadelphia 4
April 22	Philadelphia 3 at New Jersey 0

Philadelphia wins best-of-seven 4-1

Boston (6) vs. Buffalo (3)

April 15	Boston 1 at Buffalo 2
April 17	Boston 5 at Buffalo 3
April 19	Buffalo 1 at Boston 2
April 21	Buffalo 2 at Boston 3 (Satan 27:41 OT)
April 23	Boston 1 at Buffalo 4
April 26	Buffalo 3 at Boston 4

Boston wins best-of-seven 4-2

Ottawa (5) vs. Pittsburgh (4)

April 14	Ottawa 5 at Pittsburgh 4
April 16	Ottawa 1 at Pittsburgh 2
April 18	Pittsburgh 4 at Ottawa 2
April 20	Pittsburgh 7 at Ottawa 4
April 22	Ottawa 4 at Pittsburgh 3 (Carkner 47:06 OT)
April 24	Pittsburgh 4 at Ottawa 3 (Dupuis 9:56 OT)

Pittsburgh wins best-of-seven 4-2

WESTERN CONFERENCE QUARTER-FINAL

Colorado (8) vs. San Jose (1)

April 14	Colorado 2 at San Jose 1
April 16	Colorado 5 at San Jose 6 (Setoguchi 5:22 OT)
April 18	San Jose 0 at Colorado 1 (R. O'Reilly 0:51) [Anderson]
April 20	San Jose 2 at Colorado 1 (Pavelski 10:24 OT)
April 22	Colorado 0 at San Jose 5 [Nabokov]
April 24	San Jose 5 at Colorado 2

San Jose wins best-of-seven 4-2

Nashville (7) vs. Chicago (2)

April 16	Nashville 4 at Chicago 1
April 18	Nashville 0 at Chicago 2 [Niemi]
April 20	Chicago 1 at Nashville 4
April 22	Chicago 3 at Nashville 0 [Niemi]
April 24	Nashville 4 at Chicago 5 (Hossa 4:07 OT)
April 26	Chicago 5 at Nashville 3

Chicago wins best-of-seven 4-2

Los Angeles (6) vs. Vancouver (3)

April 15	Los Angeles 2 at Vancouver 3 (Samuelsson 8:52 OT)
April 17	Los Angeles 3 at Vancouver 2 (Kopitar 7:28 OT)
April 19	Vancouver 3 at Los Angeles 5
April 21	Vancouver 6 at Los Angeles 4
April 23	Los Angeles 2 at Vancouver 7
April 25	Vancouver 4 at Los Angeles 2

Vancouver wins best-of-seven 4-2

Detroit (5) vs. Phoenix (4)

April 14	Detroit 2 at Phoenix 3
April 16	Detroit 7 at Phoenix 4
April 18	Phoenix 4 at Detroit 2
April 20	Phoenix 0 at Detroit 3 [Howard]
April 23	Detroit 4 at Phoenix 1
April 25	Phoenix 5 at Detroit 2
April 27	Detroit 6 at Phoenix 1

Detroit wins best-of-seven 4-3

EASTERN CONFERENCE SEMI-FINAL

Montreal (8) vs. Pittsburgh (4)

April 30   Montreal 3 at Pittsburgh 6
May 2   Montreal 3 at Pittsburgh 1
May 4   Pittsburgh 2 at Montreal 0 [Marc-Andre Fleury]
May 6   Pittsburgh 2 at Montreal 3
May 8   Montreal 1 at Pittsburgh 2
May 10   Pittsburgh 3 at Montreal 4
May 12   Montreal 5 at Pittsburgh 2

Montreal wins best-of-seven 4-3

Philadelphia (7) vs. Boston (6)

May 1   Philadelphia 4 at Boston 5 (Savard 13:52 OT)
May 3   Philadelphia 2 at Boston 3
May 5   Boston 4 at Philadelphia 1
May 7   Boston 4 at Philadelphia 5 (Gagne 14:40 OT)
May 10   Philadelphia 4 at Boston 0 [Boucher/Leighton]
May 12   Boston 1 at Philadelphia 2
May 12   Philadelphia 4 at Boston 3

Philadelphia wins best-of-seven 4-3

WESTERN CONFERENCE SEMI-FINAL

Detroit (5) vs. San Jose (1)

April 29   Detroit 3 at San Jose 4
May 2   Detroit 3 at San Jose 4
May 4   San Jose 4 at Detroit 3 (Marleau 7:07 OT)
May 6   San Jose 1 at Detroit 7
May 8   Detroit 1 at San Jose 2

San Jose wins best-of-seven 4-1

Vancouver (3) vs. Chicago (2)

May 1   Vancouver 5 at Chicago 1
May 3   Vancouver 2 at Chicago 4
May 5   Chicago 5 at Vancouver 2
May 7   Chicago 7 at Vancouver 4
May 9   Vancouver 3 at Chicago 1
May 11   Chicago 5 at Vancouver 1

Chicago wins best-of-seven 4-2

EASTERN CONFERENCE FINAL

Montreal (8) vs. Philadelphia (7)

May 16   Montreal 0 at Philadelphia 6 [Leighton]
May 18   Montreal 0 at Philadelphia 3 [Leighton]
May 20   Philadelphia 1 at Montreal 5
May 22   Philadelphia 3 at Montreal 0 [Leighton]
May 24   Montreal 2 at Philadelphia 4

Philadelphia wins best-of-seven 4-1

WESTERN CONFERENCE FINAL

Chicago (2) vs. San Jose (1)

May 16   Chicago 2 at San Jose 1
May 18   Chicago 4 at San Jose 2
May 21   San Jose 2 at Chicago 3 (Byfuglien 12:24 OT)
May 23   San Jose 2 at Chicago 4

Chicago wins best-of-seven 4-0

STANLEY CUP FINAL

May 29   Philadelphia 5 at Chicago 6
May 31   Philadelphia 1 at Chicago 2
June 2   Chicago 3 at Philadelphia 4
June 4   Chicago 3 at Philadelphia 5
June 6   Philadelphia 4 at Chicago 7
June 9   Chicago 4 at Philadelphia 3 (Kane 4:06 OT)

Chicago wins Stanley Cup 4-2

	GP	G	A	P	Pim
Jonathan Toews	22	7	22	29	4
Patrick Kane	22	10	18	28	6
Patrick Sharp	22	11	11	22	16
Duncan Keith	22	2	15	17	10
Dustin Byfuglien	22	11	5	16	20
Dave Bolland	22	8	8	16	30
Marian Hossa	22	3	12	15	25
Kris Versteeg	22	6	8	14	14
Brent Seabrook	22	4	7	11	14
Troy Brouwer	19	4	4	8	8
Niklas Hjalmarsson	22	1	7	8	6
Tomas Kopecky	17	4	2	6	8
Andrew Ladd	19	3	3	6	12
Brent Sopel	22	1	5	6	8
Brian Campbell	19	1	4	5	2
Ben Eager	18	1	2	3	20
John Madden	22	1	1	2	2
Bryan Bickell	4	0	1	1	2
Antti Niemi	22	0	0	0	2
Adam Burish	15	0	0	0	2
Jordan Hendry	15	0	0	0	2
Nick Boynton	3	0	0	0	2
Colin Fraser	3	0	0	0	0
Cristobal Huet	1	0	0	0	0

In Goal	GP	W-L	Mins	GA	SO	GAA
Antti Niemi	22	16-6	1,321:51	58	2	2.63
Cristobal Huet	1	0-0	19:56	0	0	0.00

The Blackhawks pour off the ice after beating Philadelphia 2-1 in Game Two of the Stanley Cup Final.

By Draft

Bryan Bickell
Drafted 41st overall by Chicago in 2004

Adam Burish
Drafted 282nd overall by Chicago in 2002

Jonathan Toews
Drafted 3rd overall by Chicago in 2006

Patrick Kane
Drafted 1st overall by Chicago in 2007

Dustin Byfuglien
Drafted 245th overall by Chicago in 2003

Dave Bolland
Drafted 32nd overall by Chicago in 2004

Duncan Keith
Drafted 54th overall by Chicago in 2002

Brent Seabrook
Drafted 14th overall by Chicago in 2003

Niklas Hjalmarsson
Drafted 108th overall by Chicago in 2005

Troy Brouwer
Drafted 214th overall by Chicago in 2004

By Free Agent Signing

Jordan Hendry
Signed as a free agent by Chicago on July 17, 2006

Antti Niemi
Signed as a free agent by Chicago on May 5, 2008

Marian Hossa
Signed as a free agent by Chicago on July 1, 2009

Tomas Kopecky
Signed as a free agent by Chicago on July 1, 2009

Brent Sopel
Signed as a free agent by Chicago on October 3, 2007

Brian Campbell
Signed as a free agent by Chicago on July 1, 2008

John Madden
Signed as a free agent by Chicago on July 2, 2009

Cristobal Huet
Signed as a free agent by Chicago on July 1, 2008

By Trade

Patrick Sharp
Acquired on December 5, 2005, with Eric Meloche from Philadelphia for Matt Ellison and a 3rd-round draft choice in 2006

Kris Versteeg
Acquired on February 3, 2007, from Boston for future considerations

Andrew Ladd
Acquired February 26, 2008, from Carolina for Tuomo Ruutu

Ben Eager
Acquired on December 18, 2007, from Philadelphia for Jim Vandermeer

Colin Fraser
Acquired on February 19, 2004, with Jim Vandermeer and a 2nd-round draft choice in 2004 from Philadelphia for Alexei Zhamnov and a 4th-round draft choice in 2004

Cristobal Huet is one of eight Blackhawks who joined the team via free agency.

Acquired from Boston for nothing more than future considerations, Kris Versteeg has been one of the team's greatest acquisitions.

Rockford IceHogs, 2009-10 Regular Season Stats

Player	GP	G	A	P	Pim
Mark Cullen	62	21	32	53	16
Bracken Kearns	80	15	36	51	99
Jack Skille	63	23	26	49	50
Kyle Greentree	64	25	20	45	57
Pete MacArthur	71	8	34	42	33
Matt Keith	69	21	20	41	27
Richard Petiot	80	8	29	37	88
Brian Connelly	78	34	31	35	28
Bryan Bickell	65	16	15	31	58
Evan Brophey	79	14	17	31	39
Rob Klinkhammer	72	10	13	23	38
Jake Dowell	78	7	16	23	96
Danny Bois	73	10	12	22	156
Daryl Boyle	52	4	16	20	29
Akim Aliu	48	11	6	17	69
Nathan Davis	23	8	3	11	10
Mike Brennan	72	3	6	9	113
Jassen Cullimore	59	2	6	8	52
Simon Danis-Pepin	38	1	7	8	10
Adam Hobson	31	2	5	7	42
David Phillips	52	0	6	6	52
Danny Richmond	15	0	6	6	31
Derek Nesbitt	23	4	1	5	6
Ryan Flinn	20	2	2	4	74
Shawn Lalonde	8	1	1	2	11
Brandon Bollig	3	1	1	2	7
Bryan Ewing	9	1	1	2	4
Corey Crawford	45	0	2	2	4
Jonathan Carlsson	19	1	0	1	8
Nick Boynton	6	0	1	1	18
Maxime Tanguay	5	0	1	1	2
Jean-Claude Sawyer	4	0	1	1	2
Ryan Stanton	2	0	1	1	0
David Gilbert	1	0	1	1	0
Kyle Hagel	9	0	0	0	36
Dan Cloutier	3	0	0	0	10
Joe Falon	29	0	0	0	2
Alec Richards	6	0	0	0	0
Hannu Toivonen	6	0	0	0	0
Kyle Beach	4	0	0	0	0
Joe Charlebois	2	0	0	0	0

In Goal	GP	W-L-SOL	Mins	GA	SO	GAA
Dan Cloutier	3	1-1-0	146	6	0	2.47
Joe Fallon	29	15-10-1	1,545	68	1	2.64
Corey Crawford	45	24-16-2	2,521	112	1	2.67
Alec Richards	6	3-2-0	307	16	0	3.12
Hannu Toivonen	6	1-4-0	296	17	0	3.44

Goalie Corey Crawford was the team's top goalie in Rockford, but also got into a game in the NHL for the Blackhawks in 2009-10.

Troy Brouwer is one of many current Blackhawks who spent time with the AHL's Rockford IceHogs before making it to the NHL.

STANLEY CUP PLAYOFFS 2010

***GAME ONE** — April 16, 2010*

Nashville 4 at Chicago 1 *(Nashville leads series 1-0)*

The Predators played a perfect road game and the Hawks had trouble generating offense against their defensive-minded opponents, and the result was a surprising 4-1 loss by Chicago. The score was inflated by two empty-net goals in the final minute, but nonetheless the Hawks managed just a single goal and 26 shots.

"They play their system great," said Hawks' forward John Madden. "They're well-coached. They don't take many penalties. They're very responsible on the ice and play a very frustrating style. They played their game. They had no problem entering the third period down 1-0."

Pekka Rinne was excellent in goal for the Predators. He robbed Patrick Sharp on a breakaway in the first period, and despite Chicago's big bodies going hard to the net remained poised. Sharp had another great

Chicago's Dave Bolland intercepts a pass and tries to gain control of the puck.

Jonathan Toews controls the puck behind the Nashville net while being pursued by Predators' defenceman Dan Hamhuis.

Conference Quarter-final—Chicago Blackhawks vs. Nashville Predators

35

chance early in the second, but although he beat Rinne with a one-timer on his off wing, the puck rattled off the post and stayed out.

Indeed, Chicago's only goal came in the second period off a rebound. Nashville was caught on a turnover at the Chicago blue line, and on the ensuing odd-man rush Sharp took a shot that Rinne stopped. But with two other Hawks charging toward the net, the goalie took his eye off the puck for a split second and it fell loose. Patrick Kane knocked it in at 9:43 for the opening goal of the series.

Antti Niemi was solid in goal for Chicago, but early in the third period he coughed up a weak goal on a strange play. The puck rolled into the Chicago end along the right boards and J.P. Dumont, a left-hand shot, flipped a backhand toward the net. Defenceman

Duncan Keith swatted at the puck and got a piece of it, and it bounced weirdly past Niemi and in to tie the game.

Midway through the period the Predators got the goal they needed. Troy Brouwer gave the puck up at his own blue line and David Legwand walked in alone. Niemi made the original save, but in the ensuing scramble Dumont lifted the puck in at 10:37 for the 2-1 lead.

"The third period was a tough one," coach Joel Quenneville admitted. "We lost a bit of our momentum on (the first goal), but the second one was a tough one to give up. We had possession, had fresh legs, and turned it over in a critical spot."

Two empty-netters finished the scoring, and the capacity crowd in Chicago went home disappointed.

Members of the Chicago Cubs don Blackhawks' sweaters while watching from a private box.

Goalie Antti Niemi maintains his balance and composure as teammates come to his aid.

GAME TWO — *April 18, 2010*

Nashville 0 at **Chicago 2** *(Series tied 1-1)*

The playoffs would not have started well had the heavily-favoured Hawks lost the first two home games in the first round. A win was critical on this night, and they knew it.

As in Game One, Chicago dominated the first two periods, but Predators' goalie Pekka Rinne was both sensational and lucky. He made back-to-back saves early in the first off Tomas Kopecky and Marian Hossa, but then Jonathan Toews had him down and out and hit the crossbar. Hossa had threaded the pass through several players in front to get Toews the puck to the back side of the play.

"We had quite a few chances like that one that hit the bar in the first period, but you can't let that type of thing get to you," Toews said later. "You've just got to keep working and make something happen."

The scoreless first period gave way to more offense in the second, and Antti Niemi was also sharp in the Chicago net, making a sensational right-pad save off Dustin Boyd. Moments later, seemingly down and out, Niemi reached out with his glove to stop a sure Boyd goal.

Midway through the period, David Bolland gave the Hawks a 1-0 lead on the power play. Toews got the puck at the top of the crease and made a sensational blind pass behind him to Bolland coming in on goal. Bolland roofed a backhand over a surprised Rinne who had no idea the puck was going to the back side on that play.

Later in the period Rinne made another great stop off Hossa, diving across the crease to block a sure goal. Like Game One, the Hawks started the third having a huge advantage in play but only the slimmest of leads. This night, though, there was no letting up. Dan Hamhuis made an unwise pinch at the Chicago blue line after David Legwand was stripped of the puck by Patrick Kane, and Kane broke out down the right wing on a three-on-one. He waited and made a perfect shot to the far side, and the 2-0 lead was all the Hawks needed.

"You get that second goal and everyone's just a little looser and you play with more confidence," said Kane. "We came out with a couple of bad shifts [in the third], but we turned it around and played well the rest of the game."

Vince Vaughn and wife Kyla Weber take in the action at the United Center.

Nashville's Ryan Suter tries to keep Jonathan Toews at bay as they fight for the puck along the boards.

Chicago's Andrew Ladd (middle) tries to make some space for himself while Nashville's Francis Bouillon keeps an eye on action in the corner.

The Blackhawks salute their fans in European fashion after winning Game Two on home ice.

Conference Quarter-final—Chicago Blackhawks vs. Nashville Predators

GAME THREE — *April 20, 2010*
Chicago 1 at Nashville 4 *(Nashville leads series 2-1)*

For the second time in the series it was Nashville that took the lead, thanks again to great defence against Chicago's top duo of Jonathan Toews and Patrick Kane. Goalie Pekka Rinne was outstanding as well, and the Hawks were left wondering how their high-powered offense had managed just four goals in the first three games.

The Predators got off to a great start on two counts. First, defenceman Shea Weber hammered Patrick Kane along the boards.

"I think it got the crowd involved, got us kind of fired up and with a guy like that who already has scored in back-to-back games against us it was good to shut him down a little bit," Nashville forward Joel Ward said.

Moments later, Rinne made a great pad save on a partial breakaway by Kris Versteeg. Francis Bouillon then nailed Colin Fraser with a hard but clean check. The only flaw for the Preds was two puck-handling errors by Rinne that resulted in great scoring chances, but the Hawks failed to capitalize.

Not to be outdone, Antti Niemi made a fine stop on a David Legwand breakaway at the other end of the ice. So many scoring chances had to produce a goal at some point, and that came at the 13:00 mark, when Joel Ward knocked in a rebound after Niemi stopped the initial shot from Steve Sullivan.

A few minutes later, the Hawks scored to tie the game, on a power play. Hossa took a shot that was lightly deflected by Versteeg in front, and the puck landed on the stick of Tomas Kopecky off to the side. He easily back-handed it in the open side with less than three minutes left in the period.

Patrick Sharp is hounded by Kevin Klein as the puck rolls along the boards.

Despite the acrobatic goaltending of Antti Niemi and help from Dustin Byfuglien, Joel Ward of Nashville manages to lift the puck in.

Just four minutes into the second, the Predators collected a lead they never relinquished. Sullivan took a breakout pass to create a two-on-one, and he fed Legwand perfectly going to the net. Legwand redirected the puck over the outstretched blocker of Niemi to make it 2-1.

Six minutes later, Weber, who has the hardest shot in the game, made it a two-goal lead for the home team. He smashed a rolling puck from the blue line that deflected off Hossa in front and went in under Niemi.

The final goal of the game came in the later stages of the third period after Dustin Byfuglien hooked Martin Erat on a break. Erat was awarded a penalty shot, and he drilled a hard snap shot over the glove of Niemi, the first playoff penalty shot goal in franchise history.

"It wasn't bad, but I really thought we lost all momentum in that second period," Chicago coach Joel Quenneville said of his team's effort. "Then they took the game over. The building was alive and had some personality and we put ourselves in the position we're in but we needed to get better off the first period's level and we weren't there."

Conference Quarter-final—Chicago Blackhawks vs. Nashville Predators

41

Tomas Kopecky celebrates his goal to tie the score, 1-1, in the first period.

Conference Quarter-final—Chicago Blackhawks vs. Nashville Predators

GAME FOUR — *April 22, 2010*

Chicago 3 at Nashville 0 *(Series tied 2-2)*

Antti Niemi stopped 33 shots for the shutout, and coach Joel Quenneville juggled his lineup a bit to inspire the Hawks to their second shutout win, a 3-0 gem to even the series and reclaim home-ice advantage. Trying to get some offense from Jonathan Toews and Patrick Kane, Quenneville put the pair together with Bryan Bickell, a big player who could get physical.

For the third time in four games Chicago got the opening goal, and it proved to be a huge one. It was Bickell who had a hand in that critical play. He drove hard to the net before being hauled down by the much smaller Nashville defenceman Francis Bouillon, and on the ensuing power play Patrick Sharp whacked the puck over the goal line in a wild scramble around Pekka Rinne's crease. The goal came just ten seconds after the Bouillon penalty.

The Predators had a great chance to tie the game later in the period when they had an extended five-on-three, but they couldn't get a big slapshot from Shea Weber on goal and later incurred a penalty of their own.

Chicago's huge forward Dustin Byfuglien outmuscles the much smaller Steve Sullivan behind the Predators' goal.

Goalie Antti Niemi focuses on the game.

"We shot a lot of pucks but we didn't get them through or we missed the net or went over the net," Predators' coach Barry Trotz said. "Just as a power-play goal can give you momentum, a big penalty kill or a big save will give you momentum. I'm pretty sure they got some momentum off that."

The Blackhawks got the all-important second goal off the rush at 12:55 of the second period. Marian Hossa skated down the right wing into the Nashville end and lost the puck in his skates. The Predators relaxed for a split second, sensing they had a chance to recover, but Hossa quickly shot on goal and Rinne failed to handle the shot. Toews was right there and knocked the loose puck into the open side of the net for a 2-0 road lead.

Dan Hamhuis (left) and Tomas Kopecky engage in a spirited battle for the puck in open ice.

The back-breaker came with less than four minutes remaining in the second. Again the goal came off the rush, and again it seemed like a play in which nothing would happen. Patrick Sharp skated in over the blue line, cut to the middle, and used defenceman Bouillon as a screen. His shot against the grain beat Rinne to the blocker side, and with the score 3-0 the Predators were unable to mount a comeback.

"Everybody had a good game across the board," said Quenneville. "Sharp scored a huge goal there to make it 3-0. We had the puck a little more. All four lines contributed."

Patrick Sharp (#10) and teammates celebrate the first goal of the game, the eventual game winner.

Conference Quarter-final—Chicago Blackhawks vs. Nashville Predators

45

GAME FIVE — *April 24, 2010*

Nashville 4 at **Chicago 5** (OT)

(Chicago leads series 3-2)

From goat to hero in the course of minutes: few playoff games have ever had such incredible changes of fortunes as this for Chicago's Marian Hossa. The team blew a 3-1 lead and found itself trailing 4-3 as time wound down, and the game seemed lost when Hossa took a five-minute major for boarding with only 1:03 left in regulation.

Amazingly, the Hawks tied the game with only 13.6 seconds left thanks to a short-handed goal by Patrick Kane, and then, in overtime, Hossa stepped out of the penalty box and scored the game winner at 4:07 to give the Hawks a crucial 3-2 lead in the series.

"What a relief," said Hossa afterwards. "It was one of the longest I've ever sat in the penalty box, especially in a big game like this. Luckily the rebound came to me, so I just put it in. The guys on the PK deserve lots of credit. I was jumping in the box like a little kid when I saw there were only a few seconds left (in the penalty). I couldn't think of a better ending than this."

Hawks' fans might say the game never should have come down to a last-minute penalty in the first place, given how the team dominated the first 40 minutes, outshooting Nashville 24-8 and having a commensurate edge in play.

The Predators did score the first goal early in the game, though, thanks to David Legwand. The lefty shot claimed a loose puck along the right boards and snapped a quick shot off his back skate that beat Antti Niemi off the far post.

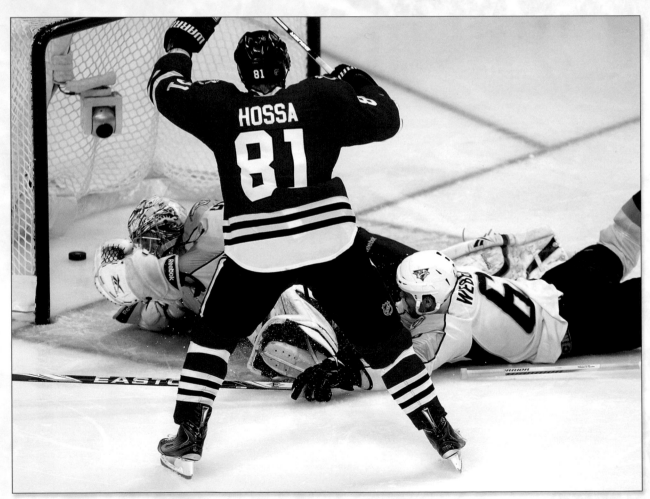

Marian Hossa scores the game winner in overtime as goalie Pekka Rinne and defenceman Shea Weber try in vain to make the save.

(page 47) Chicago defenceman Brent Seabrook clears the puck from the side of the goal.

46

Conference Quarter-final—Chicago Blackhawks vs. Nashville Predators

Conference Quarter-final—Chicago Blackhawks vs. Nashville Predators

47

Tomas Kopecky (left) and Jonathan Toews hug after Kopecky scored to make it a 3-1 game.

The Hawks took over soon after and tied the game midway through the period. Brent Seabrook's quick shot from the point was stopped by Pekka Rinne, but Andrew Ladd scooped in the rebound before Ryan Suter could check him in time.

Chicago went ahead before the end of the period on a similar play. Niklas Hjalmarsson took a shot from the point. This time it went through several players in front and beat Rinne cleanly. The 2-1 score was deserved by the Hawks given their territorial advantage during the period.

Chicago kept the heat on in the second period, pumping shots at Rinne. At one point late in the period, shots were 20-5 in Chicago's favour, and they upped their lead to 3-1 on a weird play. Tomas Kopecky came out of the penalty box and claimed a clearing, waltzed in on goal and outfought Suter, beating Rinne with a deke just as the goalie was trying to make a pokecheck. This gave the home side a two-goal lead.

The Hawks couldn't take the lead to the dressing room, though. Kane gave the puck up in the Nashville end and David Legwand carried it out on a two-on-one with Joel Ward. They played the set-up perfectly,

and Ward had only to redirect Legwand's pass to the far side to make it 3-2.

Early in the third, the visitors tied the score thanks to a Martin Erat shot in the slot, and at 11:39 Hawks fans were stunned when Erat scored again to put Nashville up 4-3. That set up a wild finish. With just seconds left on the clock and Nashville on the power play, Toews got the puck and carried it into the Predators end. The puck came loose on a scramble in front, and Kane knocked in the rebound to tie the game at 19:46.

"Nothing tops it," Kane said of his goal, when asked if that was the biggest goal of his young career. "Sharpie said he couldn't catch me after I scored because I was flying. That's why you play the game.... That's why hockey's such a great game. You never know what can happen."

In the overtime, Hossa atoned for his egregious error as soon as he got out of the penalty box. Play was in the Nashville end so he joined the attack. Brent Sopel took a point shot that was partially blocked in front, and Hossa was right there to flip the rebound past Rinne for the overtime victory and a decisive 3-2 series lead.

"We're sitting here now smiling about it, but we nearly let that one slip," John Madden said philosophically. "I think that's the biggest thing we've got to take from this. We have to be ready on Monday."

Nashville goalie Pekka Rinne keeps his eye on the puck as Andrew Ladd tries to deflect a shot.

Patrick Kane dives to clear the puck into the Predators' end.

GAME SIX — *April 26, 2010*
Chicago 5 at Nashville 3 *(Chicago wins series 4-2)*

There aren't many games as odd as this series-clinching one that saw the teams combine for seven first-period goals and then not another until the final minute of the game into an empty net. But the truth is that Chicago was the better team in the series and was relentless on offence to the point that it seemed only a matter of time before they cracked the Predators' defence-first style of play.

On this night, it was a power-play goal from captain Jonathan Toews near the end of the first period that held up as the winner, though as always Nashville showed an admirable resistance, battling back from a 3-1 deficit for the second straight game.

"It just seemed like Nashville wouldn't go away," said John Madden. "You've got to tip your cap to them. They just kept coming and coming and coming. And all of their guys played well. They didn't have any passengers any night."

The scoring started at 6:38 of the opening period when a routine point shot from Duncan Keith eluded everyone in front, including goalie Pekka Rinne, and found the back of the net. Two minutes later, Nashville tied the score on a similar play. Jordan Tootoo fed Shea Weber at the point, and although Weber has a deadly slapshot he elected to get off a quick wrist shot. It also eluded several bodies in front and snuck by Antti Niemi in the Chicago goal.

A minute later, the Hawks got a truly lucky goal. Off a faceoff outside the Nashville blue line, defenceman Brent Seabrook fired the puck into the Nashville end. Rinne went behind the goal to play the puck, but he didn't see that the shoot-in had hit the foot of Patrick Kane at the line and changed direction. It went directly into the empty Nashville net for a most fortunate 2-1 Blackhawks lead.

Conference Quarter-final—Chicago Blackhawks vs. Nashville Predators

49

Patrick Sharp made it a 3-1 lead off a nice rush by Marian Hossa. Hossa won a fight for the puck with defenceman Dan Hamhuis and tried a wraparound, and Sharp had a couple of cracks at it before bouncing it over Rinne. The period was far from over, however.

Jason Arnott collected a rebound on the power play at 15:44 to cut the Chicago lead to a single goal. It was the team's first man-advantage goal in the series. The Predators tied the game late in the period on a play that started with a huge hit by Hamhuis on Dustin Byfuglien, one of the biggest players in the league. Play moved up ice, and Hamhuis got off a point shot that eluded Niemi with just 54.1 seconds left, making the score 3-3.

Seconds later, though, the Predators' Jerred Smithson took a penalty and paid the price. Toews scooped up a rebound in front after Rinne failed to snare a Patrick Sharp point shot.

"Sometimes you get a break like that," coach Joel Quenneville noted. "You know, had a nice little momentum thing but the next thing you know it's 3-3. We didn't take advantage of it the way we should've or could've. But at the same time the fourth goal was a huge one."

This offensive explosion was all the scoring in the game save for an empty-netter by John Madden with eight seconds remaining. Chicago had eliminated the Predators, but it hadn't been easy.

Patrick Sharp tries to get his stick on a loose puck while being hounded by two Nashville defencemen.

Goalie Antti Niemi makes a save with the help of defenceman Duncan Keith as two Nashville players try to whack the puck in from close range.

Conference Quarter-final—Chicago Blackhawks vs. Nashville Predators

51

GAME ONE — *May 1, 2010*
Vancouver 5 at Chicago 1 *(Vancouver leads series 1-0)*

Once again the Hawks failed to use home-ice advantage to their benefit at the start of a series, and this time it was the Vancouver Canucks that ripped open a close game early on to take command and win easily, 5-1. The difference was goalie Roberto Luongo, who kept the Canucks in the game in the first few minutes, when Chicago had its greatest pressure, and then the scorers, who opened the floodgates late in the first period and early in the second.

Christian Ehrhoff started the scoring at 13:51 thanks to some determined work by Mason Raymond in the corner. Raymond won a battle for the puck against Brent Sopel and spotted Ehrhoff at the top of the circle. His quick shot to the far side beat Antti Niemi for the 1-0 Vancouver lead.

The Hawks had a great chance to tie the game when Patrick Kane had a breakaway. He was bettered by Luongo, and then on another chance, Kane had a wide-open net but missed the easy shot.

"It's a shot I've got to bury," Kane admitted, "but the puck came out so quick and it was bouncing. I think I just got behind the puck and shot it wide."

The Hawks suffered a huge blow in the final minute. Niemi made an easy save from a corner shot but kicked the rebound out to the high slot and Raymond hammered a quick drive over Niemi. It was a soft play by the goalie, and with just eleven seconds left in the period it sent the Hawks to the dressing room demoralized.

The back-breaker came early in the second. The Sedin twins danced around the Chicago net creating several great chances, and although Niemi was heroic, Henrik Sedin finally buried the puck just 32 seconds into the period to make it 3-0.

Captain Jonathan Toews is closely checked by Alexander Edler.

Goalie Roberto Luongo makes the save while Dustin Byfuglien looks for the rebound.

No fewer than half a dozen players clog the area in front of Roberto Luongo, making it difficult for the goalie to follow the puck.

Conference Semi-final—Chicago Blackhawks vs. Vancouver Canucks

"That last goal at the end of the first period and that first goal at the beginning of the second period, that maybe took a little bit of the momentum away from them," Vancouver coach Alain Vigneault noted.

Midway through the second period, the Canucks made it 4-0 on a similar play—the result of extended possession in the Chicago end more than a play off the rush. Ehrhoff's point shot was stopped by Niemi, but in the ensuing scramble Kyle Wellwood pushed the puck over the line before the net came off its moorings. A goal late in the period by Michael Grabner made it 5-0. The Hawks got their only goal early in the third on a two-man advantage. By this point, Niemi was on the bench in favour of Cristobal Huet.

"I'm not blaming the goaltending at all," Hawks' coach Joel Quenneville said. "They were around the net and had second and third opportunities. That's an area we need help, and that's an area we need to be better."

Brent Sopel tries awkwardly to make a play while on one knee.

Tomas Kopecky is checked by Vancouver's Kevin Bieksa just inside the Canucks' blue line.

GAME TWO — *May 3, 2010*
Vancouver 2 at **Chicago 4** *(Series tied 1-1)*

As they had in the first series against Nashville, Chicago rallied for a win in a game the team just had to win. The Hawks stumbled to start but scored the only three goals of the third period to beat Vancouver, 4-2, and even their best-of-seven series 1-1.

"It's a big win," Patrick Sharp said. "We've got a big one coming up in Game 3. It's going to be a good series; it's going to be a long one. We'll enjoy this one tonight."

The Canucks struck early, with Mason Raymond opening the scoring at 1:22 of the first period. A loose puck came back to the point, and although Antti Niemi made the original save, Raymond roofed the rebound over the goalie for the early 1-0 lead.

Niemi made a huge pad save on Kevin Bieksa only moments later, but the Canucks made it 2-0 during a two-man advantage. Henrik Sedin flipped a perfect pass through the crease to Mikael Samuelsson on the back side, who had only to re-direct it into the open side.

Less than three minutes later, the Hawks got on the board with a much-needed goal. Brent Seabrook snuck in from the point and took a pass in front from Dave Bolland, one-timing the puck past goalie Roberto Luongo who was still watching it behind his net.

Both goalies then controlled the game. The teams had plenty of scoring chances but couldn't beat Niemi and Luongo. Adam Burish had the best chance in the second period but was stopped on a breakaway. Kesler was then stoned by Niemi on a three-on-one short-handed break by the Canucks. It took almost 40 minutes for the next goal.

Sharp tied the game at 6:49 of the third period thanks to a poor decision by Christian Ehrhoff at the Vancouver blue line. The Canucks were on the power

Jonathan Toews (left) and Patrick Kane go to the front of the net looking for a pass.

The Blackhawks celebrate a 4-2 victory to even the series at one game each.

play but Ehrhoff pinched and lost the puck to Sharp. He skated in on a two-on-one, outwaited Luongo, and slid the puck into the open net as the goalie sprawled awkwardly.

The game seemed destined for overtime, but the Hawks had one big goal left in them. After being thwarted on another odd-man rush when Kris Versteeg held onto the puck for too long, they established possession in the Vancouver end.

Duncan Keith got the puck at the point and moved it over to Versteeg, who took dead aim at the top corner while Luongo scrambled to cover the short side. The puck went in with just 90 seconds left in regulation, and Patrick Kane closed out the scoring with an empty-netter.

"I was going to shoot it and there was like four bodies there," Versteeg said. "I wasn't too happy with myself because I thought I kind of threw it away. The puck came back and I just tried to shoot it and it went in."

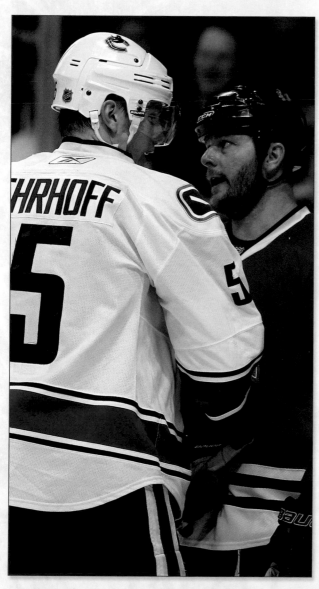

Vancouver's Christian Ehrhoff and John Madden exchange words during a stoppage in play.

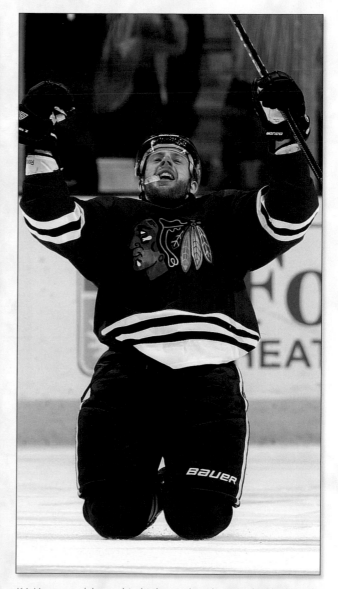

Kris Versteeg celebrates his third-period goal to give the Blackhawks a 3-2 lead.

GAME THREE — *May 5, 2010*

Chicago 5 at Vancouver 2 *(Chicago leads series 2-1)*

The Hawks got a big game from the biggest player on the team, Dustin Byfuglien, who used his weight and strength to record his first career playoff hat trick and lead the Hawks to a key road victory. All three goals were set up by captain Jonathan Toews.

"It's good to have a good start," Toews said. "We kept that effort going through three periods. It was our best effort and most complete effort of the series."

Kris Versteeg opened the scoring at 5:19 of the first period on a junk play that ended with the puck in the net. A routine point shot turned into an adventure in the crease when goalie Roberto Luongo couldn't make a clean save, and after a wild scramble Versteeg found the puck in the blue ice and pushed it over the goal line.

The Canucks had two great chances to tie the game, but Antti Niemi made huge saves on Daniel Sedin and Mikael Samuelsson. Late in the first, the Hawks made it 2-0 on another scramble when Luongo couldn't hold a point shot by Duncan Keith. This time Byfuglien whacked the loose puck home on a power play.

"When there's traffic, you know, and there are shots, sometimes it's tough to control the rebounds," Luongo explained. "Duncan Keith has a slapper from the top of the circle. I don't know how you can control a rebound like that. It squirted out. I tried to cover it and, obviously there were some sticks there whacking at it."

Vancouver cut the lead to one midway through the second period on a nice play. Alexander Edler had the puck at the point but noticed a crush of bodies in the slot so he ripped a hard pass to Jannik Hansen off to the side of the net. Hansen redirected it past Niemi to make it a 2-1 game.

Steve Bernier (#18) is stopped by the right pad of Antti Niemi, while teammate Kyle Wellwood (#42) looks on from the back side of the play.

58

Conference Semi-final—Chicago Blackhawks vs. Vancouver Canucks

The master of drama, Dustin Byfuglien celebrates one of his three goals.

Conference Semi-final—Chicago Blackhawks vs. Vancouver Canucks

59

Byfuglien got another on the power play just three minutes later, though, using his big body to get to a loose puck and flipping it over a down-and-out Luongo. Alexandre Burrows cut the lead to one in the final minute with a quick shot in the slot, but that was as close as the Canucks were to come this night.

Marian Hossa got the fourth goal midway through the third period on another rebound. Luongo failed to handle a routine shot from Patrick Sharp, and Hossa claimed the puck and slid it home past a helpless goalie. Byfuglien completed his hat trick when he pushed home a pass from Toews, not even realizing the puck had crossed the line among the group of players in the crease.

"He had a big impact on the game," Chicago coach Joel Quenneville said of Byfuglien. "He was quite physical. He had a presence around the net and finished. Certainly he was a big factor."

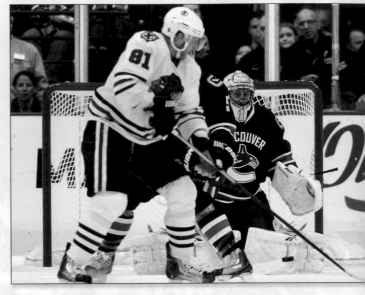

Marian Hossa tries to tip a shot directed at goalie Roberto Luongo.

Chicago's Brent Seabrook goes for a spill as Mikael Samuelsson looks on from the side of Antti Niemi's crease.

No fewer than nine players end up in the crease at the end of the play while goalie Antti Niemi calmly freezes the puck.

GAME FOUR — *May 7, 2010*
Chicago 7 at Vancouver 4 *(Chicago leads series 3-1)*

Captain Jonathan Toews had his best game of the playoffs, scoring three goals on the power play and adding two assists as Chicago crushed Vancouver and took control of the series. The Hawks won both games at GM Place and now headed home with a chance to eliminate the Canucks. Toews' five-point night, meanwhile, matched a Blackhawks' team record set by Stan Mikita in 1973 and equaled only once later, by Steve Larmer in 1990.

"It's one of those nights where you get some chances and you throw it on net and it happens to go in," said Toews. "It's nice to get those breaks. You work hard, and don't always expect to get lucky like that."

For Vancouver, the loss could be attributed to two factors—too many penalties and weak goaltending. Chicago had eight power plays and scored four goals, while Roberto Luongo continued to struggle.

"I think right now he's the second-best goaltender on the ice," Vancouver coach Alain Vigneault said of his goalie.

Chicago came out on fire, scoring the first goal just 18 seconds after the opening faceoff. Toews spotted defenceman Brent Seabrook in the high slot, and his shot beat Luongo cleanly. Just 76 seconds later, though, the Canucks tied it on a strange play. Mikael Samuelsson flipped a puck from behind the Chicago net. It hit the back of Kyle Wellwood and fell into the net without Wellwood even knowing it.

Toews did it all to get the team's second goal, this on a power play. He won the faceoff in the Vancouver end, and then headed for the slot to get open. Taking

Conference Semi-final—Chicago Blackhawks vs. Vancouver Canucks

61

Duncan Keith has a one-on-one moment with Roberto Luongo.

Tomas Kopecky and Marian Hossa celebrate a goal.

Antti Niemi makes the save with traffic in front of his crease.

a pass from Patrick Kane, he ripped a shot off the near post and in to make it 2-1 for the visitors.

Daniel Sedin tied the game again late in the opening period, but the second was all Chicago. Toews got his second of the night early on another power play. Duncan Keith slapped the puck in on a shoot-in, and as the puck rolled around the boards it went off the Ryan Kesler's stick right to Toews in the slot. His quick shot beat a surprised Luongo to make it 3-2 Chicago just 27 seconds into the period.

Patrick Sharp added a power-play goal several minutes later on another scramble in front, and then Toews completed the hat trick, converting a Dave Bolland pass in the slot, right in the middle of the Vancouver box formation, just as Kane had done for Toews in the opening period.

Vancouver got a late goal with the man advantage from Alexander Edler to make it 5-3, but the Hawks didn't let up in the final period. Tomas Kopecky added to the lead early in the third off a rebound to the back side of Luongo, and Henrik Sedin closed out the Vancouver scoring with a late goal. Bolland added the final tally into the empty net.

"You've got a lot of momentum, so we want to go home and take advantage of it," Chicago coach Joel Quenneville said. "We've got to be smart, and we've got to be disciplined. We should be excited about being back home."

Up 3-1 in the series, the Hawks had every right to be excited, but Toews cautioned otherwise. "Everyone knows that in a series, the fourth win is the toughest win to get," he said.

Michael Grabner has a great chance to score on Niemi, but the goalie makes the save.

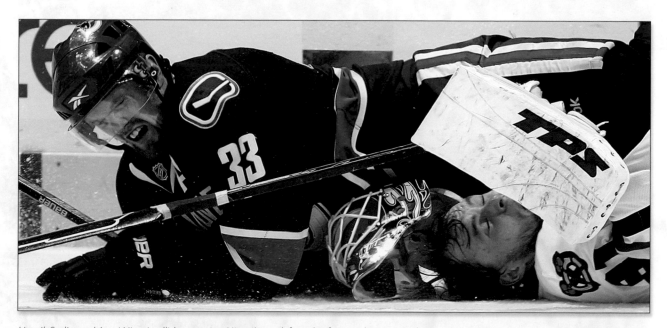

Henrik Sedin and Antti Niemi collide, wresting Niemi's mask from his face and stopping play.

Conference Semi-final—Chicago Blackhawks vs. Vancouver Canucks

63

GAME FIVE — *May 9, 2010*

Vancouver 4 at Chicago 1 *(Chicago leads series 3-2)*

Everything that went wrong for Vancouver at home went right in Chicago, and the Hawks, with a chance to end the series early and get some rest before the Conference final, failed to close out the Canucks. Vancouver took fewer penalties, came up with big plays on the penalty kill, got timely goals and great goaltending from Roberto Luongo, and played a relaxed game as Chicago tensed up. The result was a 4-1 win and chance to play another game at home.

"We're just happy to still be playing," said Canucks' defenceman Shane O'Brien. "They're a great team over there and I'm sure they'll make their adjustments, but I know when Bobby Lu [Luongo] is on like that we're a pretty good team. So we're just going to continue to play hard in front of him, and hopefully he can continue to see pucks so we can continue playing hockey."

The Canucks got the first goal of the game just 59 seconds in thanks to a seeing-eye point shot from Christian Ehrhoff. It wasn't a hard blast, but it somehow found its way past a maze of players and a screened Antti Niemi into the goal.

The Canucks made it 2-0 on a gorgeous play coming up ice. Mikael Samuelsson hit Kyle Wellwood with a pass as he skated in over the blue line to create a two-on-one, and Wellwood feathered a great pass to Kevin Bieksa, who tucked the puck in after a nice deke on Niemi.

Bieksa got his second of the game midway through the second period on a one-timer from the point. The Hawks had kept the score close despite having fewer scoring chances, but this was a debilitating goal for the home side as Chicago couldn't finish the few chances it did generate.

The Hawks did manage a goal at 12:51 of the final period to draw within two. Duncan Keith made a sensational slap-pass from the point to Toews off to

Kris Versteeg lets go a slapshot.

64

Conference Semi-final—Chicago Blackhawks vs. Vancouver Canucks

Jonathan Toews fights for the puck with Christian Ehrhoff (#5) and Kevin Bieksa.

Conference Semi-final—Chicago Blackhawks vs. Vancouver Canucks

65

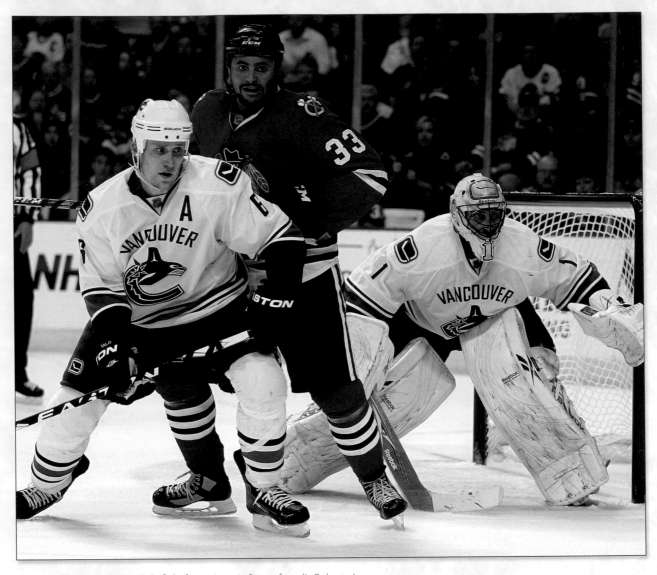

Dustin Byfuglien and Sami Salo fight for territory in front of goalie Roberto Luongo.

the side of Luongo, and Toews made a perfect tip of the puck into the net to give the Hawks a flicker of hope.

Alexandre Burrows closed out the scoring with an empty-net goal in the final minute.

"We were obviously more desperate because we were in a do-or-die situation, and we did whatever we could to kill them off," Luongo said. "We also didn't take eight penalties to be in the box all game," he added, referring to his team's lack of discipline in Game Four.

Of course, for every point of view there is a corollary, and Chicago defenceman Brian Campbell saw the game differently. "We just didn't skate near as well as we could have," he said. "We can control a lot of how we play and how we skate, and we didn't move the puck. They're a great team, but we made them better in some areas because we didn't come through in how we were supposed to play."

GAME SIX — *May 11, 2010*

Chicago 5 at Vancouver 1 *(Chicago wins series 4-2)*

Although Chicago managed to win only one of three home games in this series, the team won all three games at GM Place in Vancouver, and as a result of their road record advanced to the Conference final against San Jose. A torrid second period was the difference in the game as Chicago blew open a scoreless game by netting the only three goals of the middle period.

"We are pretty comfortable here," Chicago forward Dave Bolland admitted. "All the guys love playing here. I don't know what it is, but it's fun."

The first period may have passed without a goal, but it wasn't for lack of effort by either team. Patrick Kane hit the post on one rush, and Mikael Samuelsson at the other end was robbed by the Hawks' Antti Niemi. Patrick Sharp was bested by Roberto Luongo on a breakaway, and the Sedin twins had a couple of good scoring chances as well.

The first goal didn't come until the two-minute mark of the second, the result of a quick outlet pass from Brent Sopel to Sharp and a perfect pass to Troy Brouwer in front. Brouwer had been in the press box earlier in the series but made the most of his chance to play, beating Kyle Wellwood to the front of the net and then roofing Sharp's pass over Luongo's glove.

Mason Raymond has a scoring chance, but on one knee he can't get off a hard shot on Antti Niemi.

Conference Semi-final—Chicago Blackhawks vs. Vancouver Canucks

67

Goalie Antti Niemi somehow maintains his balance to make a glove save while players collide all around him.

Conference Semi-final—Chicago Blackhawks vs. Vancouver Canucks

Just 36 seconds later, Chicago created a turnover at center ice to create a three-on-one, and Kris Versteeg walked in on goal and beat Luongo with a wrist shot to silence the crowd and give the Hawks a huge 2-0 lead.

The crusher came with 44.7 seconds left in the second. Pavol Demitra had the puck at the point on a Vancouver power play, but he was stripped of it by Dave Bolland. Demitra tried to harass and catch Bolland as the Hawks' forward pulled away, but Bolland managed to get off a shot that squeezed through Luongo's pads. Vancouver headed to the dressing room down 3-0 and with the dim prospect of only 20 minutes left in its season.

The Canucks did manage to get the next goal, early in the third, when Shane O'Brien's shot handcuffed Antti Niemi, but four-and-a-half minutes later Patrick Kane restored the three-goal lead when he took a pass from Jonathan Toews streaking over the blue line. Kane hesitated just a second before shooting, freezing Luongo and then finding the far side to make it a 4-1 game.

Dustin Byfuglien added a goal just 25 seconds later to ensure a crushing defeat for the Canucks, losers to the Hawks for the second straight year in the playoffs.

"Our effort wasn't good enough in Game 5," Toews said. "It's tough to win four games. You really have to battle those last couple of ones out. We didn't deserve to win that one at home [Game Five], but we showed that we obviously did tonight."

Chicago eliminated the Canucks in Game Six, and two Olympics teammates—Jonathan Toews and Roberto Luongo—shake hands.

Conference Semi-final—Chicago Blackhawks vs. Vancouver Canucks

69

CONFERENCE FINAL
Chicago Blackhawks vs. San Jose Sharks

GAME ONE — *May 16, 2010*

Chicago 2 at **San Jose 1** *(Chicago leads series 1-0)*

A nice five-day layoff was just what the Blackhawks needed before facing the top team in the Western Conference. They got a great performance from goalie Antti Niemi as well as timely scoring from Dustin Byfuglien, who was quickly becoming one of the stories of the 2010 playoffs. Although the Sharks had eight days off themselves, they were bested by a 44-save effort from the Finnish goalie in the Blackhawks' net.

Dustin Byfuglien gets props from teammates after scoring the go-ahead goal.

It didn't have to be that way. Playing at home, San Jose came out flying and scored the only goal of the opening period. Jason Demers got it on the power play, a harmless-looking wrister from just inside the blue line that sailed over the blocker arm of Niemi.

Neither the goalie nor his teammates were flustered by the goal, and try as they might, the Sharks couldn't increase their lead. Dany Heatley had a couple of great chances but couldn't beat the Niemi, and late in the period Jonathan Toews hit the post for Chicago but the puck stayed out of Evgeni Nabokov's net.

Niemi proved entirely unbeatable over the final two periods, though, and the Blackhawks remained patient, slowly working away on the Sharks' defence. Midway through the middle period, the Hawks came over the blue line on a four-on-three, and Patrick Sharp, the trailer, took a pass just inside the line and let go a quick wrist shot. The puck fooled Nabokov and slipped through his pads, a bad goal to give up at a time when his counterpart, Niemi, was playing so well.

Niemi was never better than late in the second period when the Hawks were killing off a penalty. He stopped all eight shots with San Jose's extra attacker, several the result of great puck movement by the Sharks. Ryane Clowe thought he had a goal only to watch Niemi reach back and sweep his glove across to grab the puck inches from the line.

The Hawks got the go-ahead goal at 13:15 of the third on a faceoff in the Sharks' end to the left of Nabokov. Toews won the draw, and the puck came to Patrick Kane along the boards. He moved it quickly to Byfuglien at the top of the circle, and his quick shot beat Nabokov for the critical goal of the game. It was Byfuglien's fifth goal in as many playoff games.

"We keep telling him to just hit the net and either one of the other two, Kaner or I, will go find the rebound," Toews said. "Sometimes he just has to hit the net, and he showed he can power it right through a goaltender. It doesn't matter where he is, he's hungry to score goals and we want him to keep playing that way."

The overhead camera captures the symmetric chaos around goalie Antti Niemi's crease as Brent Sopel prevents Rob Blake from scoring.

Conference Final—Chicago Blackhawks vs. San Jose Sharks

71

The Sharks mounted a fierce attack in the final minutes to try to tie the game. They had a great chance in the last minute of play with Nabokov on the bench along with a Chicago penalty. But despite the two-man advantage, Niemi stood tall and preserved the win.

"It goes to show, doesn't take much for them to score goals," San Jose coach Todd McLellan said. "They'll find a way to put it in."

Dustin Byfuglien crashes into the net while avoiding goalie Evgeni Nabokov.

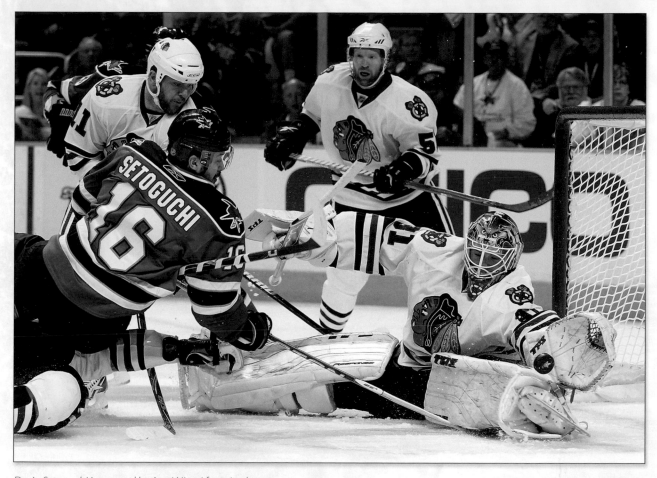

Devin Setoguchi is stopped by Antti Niemi from in close.

GAME TWO — *May 18, 2010*

Chicago 4 at San Jose 2 *(Chicago leads series 2-0)*

The Hawks continued their impressive road play by winning their seventh straight game away from the United Center, a club record that also tied the NHL record. It was done not so much because of the goaltending of Antti Niemi, as in Game One, but because of bending and not breaking at the start of the game, timely scoring, and frustrating the Sharks' top line of Dany Heatley-Patrick Marleau-Joe Thornton.

"Somehow we have to harness what we start with and continue on," San Jose coach Todd McLellan said. "We can't let little bumps in the road slow us down. I'm not sure it's about skating any faster. It's the puck movement. We don't continue to do what we started to do. We try and force it a little bit more. All of a sudden we look slower."

Indeed, the Sharks did everything but score in the first ten minutes of the game, but Niemi was sharp and the Sharks couldn't finish, and it was Chicago that scored first. Andrew Ladd skated in over the blue line and took a long wrist shot using Niclas Wallin as a screen. Goalie Evgeni Nabokov was fooled, and the Hawks silenced the HP Pavilion crowd by drawing first blood at 12:48.

Chicago made it 2-0 early in the second period. Patrick Kane got the puck in the Sharks corner on the cycle and skated in a big arc almost to the blue line before letting go a quick wrist shot. Nabokov couldn't see the play because of Dustin Byfuglien, Jonathan Toews, and two Sharks players in front, but big Byfuglien got his stick on the shot and tipped it past the helpless goalie.

A minute and a half later, the Hawks got the goal that spelled the end for the Sharks. Duncan Keith's

Conference Final—Chicago Blackhawks vs. San Jose Sharks

73

quick wrist shot from the point was re-directed in front by Toews, and again Nabokov had little chance to make the save at 8:29. Not even halfway through the game, the Hawks held a commanding 3-0 lead.

Patrick Marleau did get one back for the home side at 11:08 of the second on a power play, but the Hawks refused to allow their opponents to gain momentum from the goal. He took a pass from Thornton while moving through the high slot and fired a quick wrist shot over the glove of Niemi who couldn't get over in time to set himself.

Wallin was victimized again in the third on Chicago's fourth goal. Marian Hossa simply stripped him of the puck deep in the Sharks end and made a pass back to Niklas Hjalmarsson at the point, and his shot beat Nabokov after Troy Brouwer tipped it on the way in.

Marleau got his second of the night with less than five minutes remaining, but there was no late rally in the offing this night. The Hawks were heading home with a 2-0 lead in the series and a chance to sweep with two wins on United Center ice.

"Tonight we got a couple ugly ones in front of the net," captain Jonathan Toews conceded." If we keep doing things right, we'll keep having success."

Evgeni Nabokov is unable to stop a beautiful deflection by Dustin Byfuglien in front to give Chicago a 2-0 lead in the game.

Players jam the crease of Evgeni Nabokov as the goalie coolly holds the puck for a whistle.

Conference Final—Chicago Blackhawks vs. San Jose Sharks

75

GAME THREE — *May 21, 2010*

San Jose 2 at **Chicago 3** (OT)
(Chicago leads series 3-0)

If any game this playoffs can be said to have been a character builder for the Blackhawks, this was it. San Jose got the first goal and tied the game late in the third, but thanks to more great goaltending from Antti Niemi, who stopped 44 of 46 shots, and some poise and experience in the overtime, the Hawks pulled out a victory to take a stranglehold on the series, 3-0. Dustin Byfuglien was the hero with the overtime goal to give Chicago a 3-2 win.

"I think this year we gained some experience from what we had last year," Patrick Kane said. "We've been on a pretty good roll."

In fact, the Hawks had now won seven of their last eight games and seemed ready to get back to the Cup Final for the first time since 1992.

The Sharks thought they had scored just 1:51 into the game but video review showed that Joe Pavelski kicked the puck in. The Hawks got some energy from the non-goal and came hard at Evgeni Nabokov, but he was as impenetrable at the San Jose end as Niemi was in the Chicago end. The teams headed to the dressing room after 20 minutes in a scoreless game.

San Jose drew first blood early in the second, on a five-on-three. As the three Hawks' players collapsed around Niemi, the puck came free and Patrick Marleau buried a high shot over Niemi's glove for the critical lead at 3:58.

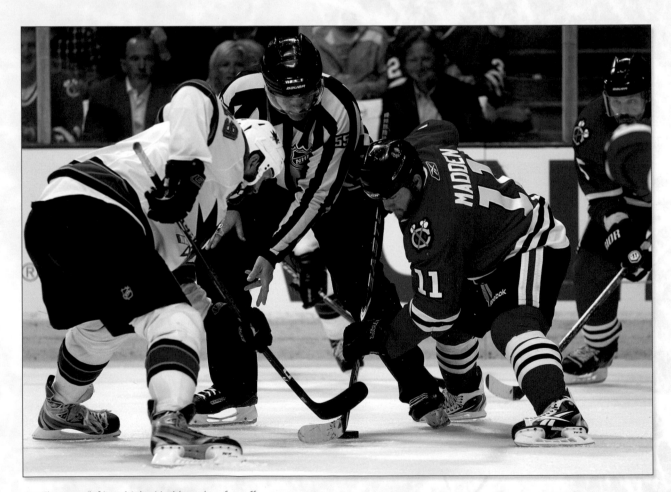

Joe Thornton (left) and John Madden take a faceoff.

Patrick Kane uses his left arm to shield his body as he skates around Marc-Eduard Vlasic of San Jose.

Three minutes later, the Hawks responded with a power-play goal of their own. This came as a result of a great pass from the right corner by Toews through the top of the crease to Patrick Sharp, who snuck in the back door and whacked the puck in before anyone on San Jose even realized he was there.

Niemi kept the score even in the third and then the Hawks scored what seemed to be the back-breaker. Dan Boyle's point shot was blocked by Toews and the puck came right to Dave Bolland at the blue line. He tore down the ice on a breakaway with Boyle giving chase, but Bolland made a nice deke and slipped the puck between Nabokov's pads to give the Hawks a 2-1 lead with only 6:55 remaining.

Marleau tied the game with his second of the night on a scramble in front with only 4:23 left in regulation, his fourth goal of five total Sharks' goals in the series. Neither team could score before the third period expired,

so they went to overtime for the first time in the series.

Dustin Byfuglien ended the game at 12:24 of the fourth period after some sustained pressure by the Hawks. Brian Campbell kept the puck in at the blue line by hammering it along the boards, and as it came behind the net Bolland got control and made a quick pass out front to Byfuglien, who was perfectly positioned between three Sharks. He ripped a one-timer under the glove of Nabokov, scoring in his fourth straight game to give the Hawks a commanding 3-0 lead in the series.

"As soon as we get away from playing our game, you know, we're a mediocre, average team," Toews said. "We got to go out there, work hard, stick to our guns, stick to how we learned to play this year. That way we're going to be tough to beat."

Despite Byfuglien's heroics, it was goalie Niemi who stood out.

Conference Final—Chicago Blackhawks vs. San Jose Sharks

77

"He's proven to a lot of people what kind of goalie he is, especially in this series," Patrick Sharp said of Niemi. "I know our captain's doing a heck of a job over there, but Antti's our MVP. He's been solid every game and hopefully it stays that way."

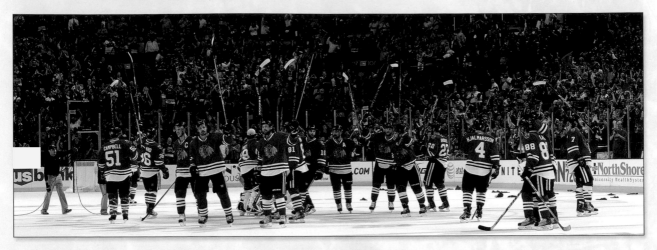

Players salute fans after a 3-2 overtime win in Game Three.

Dustin Byfuglien gets warm with the fans after scoring the game-winning goal in overtime.

78

Conference Final—Chicago Blackhawks vs. San Jose Sharks

Chicago fans anticipate a four-game sweep of the San Jose Sharks.

GAME FOUR — *May 23, 2010*
San Jose 2 at **Chicago 4** *(Chicago wins series 4-0)*

A rocky start gave way to a picture-perfect finish for the Hawks. They swept aside San Jose by rallying from two goals down midway through the game to advance to the Stanley Cup Final for the first time since 1992. It was a moment many of the young players knew would come but were impatient to experience all the same.

"It feels likes we've been together a long time," Patrick Sharp said. "A handful of guys have been here since the dark days. A group of kids that were drafted together, played in Norfolk and Rockford together. It's fun to be a part of this team on and off the ice. Guys get along so well. I think that really carries over into our play."

Victory was by no means a sure thing, even though the game was in Chicago. Logan Couture, who had been recalled eight times from the minors during the season, made it 1-0 Sharks when he wired a loose puck past Antti Niemi at 11:08 of the opening period.

The Sharks opened a 2-0 lead in the second on a strange sequence during a Chicago power play. Patrick Kane had a wide-open net to the back side of Evgeni Nabokov, but his shot was blocked by defenceman Marc-Eduard Vlasic, who saved a goal on the play. Patrick Marleau got to the puck first and cleared it away, but it hit Duncan Keith flush in the mouth. Keith skated to the bench right away and soon discovered he had lost seven teeth.

Meanwhile, the Sharks carried the puck up ice on a three-on-two, and Marleau finished the play with a one-timer on his off wing to give the visitors a huge 2-0 lead.

Dan Boyle (left) and Marian Hossa battle for the puck along the boards.

80

Conference Final—Chicago Blackhawks vs. San Jose Sharks

"I just knew right away," Keith said. "I took one breath and it felt like my whole mouth was missing, so I knew there were some teeth gone. I'm missing seven teeth now, four on the bottom and three on the top. There are no stitches, though. They're just all gone. I don't know how, but I just mashed all my teeth out. They numbed it after it happened. They stuck a bunch of needles in there and froze it all up."

Brent Seabrook brought the Hawks to within one at 13:15. He hustled down the wing and let a shot rip, and the puck landed in the crease before being inadvertently pushed over the line by Nabokov. Video review determined the puck had completely crossed the line, and Chicago was back in the game.

"We knew right away. Our report from our dressing room was it's a goal," Chicago defenceman Brian Campbell said. "We knew it. I think it was just, 'OK, let's stay calm in case anything happens.' But we were pretty positive it was going to count."

Dave Bolland tied the game with just 1:22 left in the middle period when he came out from behind the Sharks' net unchecked and lifted a shot over Nabokov's glove. The crowd was back in the game, and the Hawks were 20 minutes away from the Stanley Cup Final.

The dream came true with 5:55 left in regulation time. Kane, along the left-wing boards, saw big Dustin Byfuglien in the slot and drilled a pass that Byfuglien just redirected into the far side of the net, giving the Hawks their first lead of the night. Kris Versteeg added an empty-netter, and the Hawks had eliminated San Jose. Byfuglien counted three game-winning goals in the series.

Ever superstitious, captain Toews accepted the Clarence Campbell Bowl without touching it, and later suggested the Stanley Cup was well within reach.

"We know we can still be better," he said. "We're going to keep pushing ourselves. This is a great opportunity, a great chance. Nothing's holding us back. No reason we can't go out there and get another four wins."

Niklas Hjalmarsson celebrates a goal, but video replay showed the puck did not cross the goal line. The Blackhawks went on to win Game Four anyway and eliminate San Jose.

GAME ONE — *May 29, 2010*

Philadelphia 5 at **Chicago 6** *(Chicago leads series 1-0)*

Jonathan Toews was 18 for 24 in the faceoff circle. Chris Pronger played 32:21. Both starting goalies struggled to find the puck. The Flyers didn't incur a single penalty. It was a strange and event-filled opening game to the 2010 Stanley Cup Final at the "Madhouse on Madison."

Antti Niemi may have gotten the Hawks to the Final with his great play, but the Finnish goalie's first period was regrettably forgettable. A wild opening 20 minutes saw the Flyers head to the dressing room with a 3-2 lead thanks to three goals off rebounds.

The Flyers got the first goal—a lucky and odd one, to be sure. Ville Leino's bad angle shot was saved by Niemi's blocker, but the puck hit his own defenceman, Niklas Hjalmarsson in front, and bounced off his face and into the net. Hjalmarsson skated to the bench bloodied, but the Flyers had the first goal of the series.

The Hawks came back with two quick scores to take the lead. First, Marian Hossa made a beautiful pass from the right boards to Troy Brouwer in the high slot,

Dave Bolland's short-handed goal in the first period was part of a scoring spree by both teams.

Troy Brouwer's goal was cause for celebration by the Hawks and dejection for the four Flyers crowded around their goalie, Michael Leighton.

Stanley Cup Final—Chicago Blackhawks vs. Philadelphia Flyers

83

On his backside doing the splits, Antti Niemi keeps the puck out with a little help from defenceman Brent Sopel.

and he drilled a hard slapshot past Michael Leighton to tie the score at 7:46. Four minutes later, Dave Bolland scored short-handed. He stripped Braydon Coburn of the puck at the Hawks' blue line and walked in alone on Leighton, who got his stick on the puck but not enough to stop it from going in.

The Hawks seemed to have the momentum, but they took the only three penalties of the period and the third one finally cost them. Chris Pronger hit the post on one slapshot, and Niemi stopped another seconds later, but the rebound came out to Scott Hartnell, who lifted the puck over the sprawled goalie.

And then, with just 27 seconds left in the period, Niemi coughed up another rebound on a shot from Daniel Briere, who lifted his second shot into the top of the net to give the visitors another one-goal lead.

The goals just kept coming in the second. Patrick Sharp tied the game for Chicago on a two-on-one, faking the pass and drilling a perfect shot over the glove of Leighton. But the Hawks never got settled and never established home-ice advantage, and Blair Betts gave the Flyers another lead at 7:20.

When Niemi failed to stop a shoot-in behind the goal, Betts got the puck along the boards, moved in, fired a bad-angle shot off the far post and in. Two minutes later, though, the Hawks tied the game for the third time, with Kris Versteeg getting open in the slot and firing a quick shot past a surprised Leighton.

The Hawks took the lead for a second time thanks to a great rush from Marian Hossa. He was thwarted on the original rush but got the puck behind the Flyers' net and made a great backhand pass in front to Brouwer. He ripped a hard shot over the glove of Leighton, and that goal spelled the end of the line for the goalie as coach Peter Laviolette called in backup Brian Boucher.

The 5-4 lead failed to hold up. Hossa was responsible for a giveaway inside the Philadelphia blue line. On the ensuing rush Briere made a fine pass to Arron Asham in the slot and he drilled a one-timer past a beleaguered Niemi. The period ended 5-5 with no end in sight to the scoring spree.

The Hawks came out a different team for the third period. They attacked and forechecked and spent most of the first half in the Flyers' end—and were rewarded. Tomas Kopecky came off the bench and took a pass from Kris Versteeg in the slot. Kopecky held onto the puck, outwaited Boucher, and slid the puck in the near side to give the Hawks a 6-5 lead. They then checked Philadelphia relentlessly for the last half of the period and skated off with a crazy 6-5 victory.

84

Stanley Cup Final—Chicago Blackhawks vs. Philadelphia Flyers

GAME TWO — *May 31, 2010*

Philadelphia 1 at **Chicago 2** *(Chicago leads series 2-0)*

The Chicago Blackhawks struck for two quick goals late in the second period and rode the hot goaltending of Antti Niemi to a 2-1 win and a commanding 2-0 series lead for the Stanley Cup. It was a much more carefully played game than the opener, but the Hawks managed to find a way to win despite being outplayed.

It may have been only Game Two of a seven-game final, but it was a must-win game for Philadelphia in some ways. Since 1939, when the Cup Final went to a seven-game format, the team that jumped into a 2-0 lead won the Cup 94 per cent of the time. Furthermore, some 35 of the 40 skaters on the ice were appearing in their first Stanley Cup Final, and the nerves of Game One had settled in time for this critical match.

Philadelphia coach Peter Laviolette made two bold changes to his lineup for this game. First, he went back to goalie Michael Leighton as the starter, despite a weak outing in the first game. Second, he took out James van Riemsdyk and inserted the disruptive Daniel Carcillo. All in all, the result was a more combative and strategic first period.

The opening 20 minutes featured precious few scoring chances but plenty of drama. The Hawks made it a priority to get under the skin of defenceman Chris Pronger, who played more than 32 minutes of Game One. Leading the way was giant forward Dustin Byfuglien, and the pair slashed and whacked each other all night long. Carcillo played in the face of the Hawks as well, making for a chippy and physical first period.

Dustin Byfuglien crashes the net trying to get the puck past goalie Michael Leighton, who gets plenty of help from his teammates.

Stanley Cup Final—Chicago Blackhawks vs. Philadelphia Flyers

85

The Flyers' Dan Carcillo collides with Dustin Byfuglien, and the result has both men crashing to the ice.

Chicago did have two power plays—its first two of the series—but the Hawks couldn't muster much in the way of sustained pressure in the Flyers' end.

The second period wasn't as intense as the first, but it was just as defensive. Neither team wanted to surrender the first goal in a game clearly more cautious than the opener, but the Hawks had the edge in play at the start. Slowly but surely, though, the Flyers started to come on, generating excellent scoring chances and moving more freely into the Hawks' end. Niemi was excellent in goal, however, and the main reason the score remained 0-0 as the period wound down.

And then, seemingly out of nowhere, Chicago struck. Duncan Keith at the point found Sharp in the slot, and he took a quick shot that Leighton saved but couldn't control. Marian Hossa was right to the side of the net and swatted the puck in before Lukas Krajicek could check him, and the Hawks took a 1-0 lead. It was Hossa's first goal in more than a month.

The fans hadn't stopped cheering and the P.A. announcer hadn't even called the goal when the Hawks struck again. This time, though, it was a weak goal for Leighton. Ben Eager came down the right wing and stopped, firing a long wrist shot on goal through Matt Carle. Leighton didn't react to the play quickly, and the puck sailed in just 28 seconds after Hossa's goal for a huge Chicago 2-0 lead after 40 minutes.

The Hawks killed off an early penalty in the third, but they weren't so fortunate a few minutes later. Simon Gagne's bouncing shot in the slot hopped over Niemi's glove and into the net with just one second left on the power play, and with 14:40 left in the third period, the Flyers were right back in the game.

The goal changed the pace of the game as Philadelphia went on the attack and Chicago tried to hold onto the lead. The difference in the outcome was Niemi, who simply refused to give up the tying goal. Flyers' coach Peter Laviolette pulled Leighton with 1:44 remaining, but Philadelphia couldn't get that second goal and the teams headed to the Wachovia Center with the Blackhawks up 2-0.

The Blackhawks and Flyers get set for the opening faceoff in Game Two at the United Center.

Stanley Cup Final—Chicago Blackhawks vs. Philadelphia Flyers

87

GAME THREE — June 2, 2010
Chicago 2 at **Philadelphia 3** (OT)
(Chicago leads series 2-1)

Claude Giroux scored at 5:59 of overtime to give Philadelphia a 3-2 win in Game Three of the Stanley Cup Final. The Flyers twice held the lead in the game, but in the third period it was they who had to rally for a tie and send the game into a fourth period.

Playing on home ice, in front of a sea of orange tee-shirts, the Flyers came out as one expected, with energy and purpose. They got the only goal of the opening period on a strange power play when Chicago captain Jonathan Toews failed to clear the puck. Several players had whacks at the puck around Antti Niemi's goal, but it finally came free to Daniel Briere off to the side and he whipped it in for the 1-0 lead.

Showing typical resolve, the Hawks tied the game early in the second when Duncan Keith's shot beat Michael Leighton, but later in the period the Flyers went ahead again with the extra man. This time it was a point shot from Chris Pronger that was deflected

Dustin Byfuglien and Chris Pronger were practically joined at the hips this series. The two big men battled for position every shift.

88

Stanley Cup Final—Chicago Blackhawks vs. Philadelphia Flyers

Jonathan Toews tries to get a loose puck by Michael Leighton's crease as Mike Richards helps his goalie.

in front by Scott Hartnell. The puck inched over the line and Niklas Hjalmarsson scooped it away, Play continued for 90 seconds until the next whistle, after which video review confirmed the puck had, indeed, crossed the goal line.

Again, though, the Hawks fought back, and at 17:52 they tied the game. John Madden won a faceoff in the Philadelphia end and Brent Sopel's quick shot from the point fooled Leighton. Teams went to the dressing room tied 2-2 after 40 minutes.

Rather than start slowly in the third for fear of giving up the big goal, both teams came out guns a-blazin', and Chicago got its first lead at 2:50 on the counter attack. The Flyers had good possession in the Chicago end, but Toews controlled the puck coming and fed Kane a breakaway pass. He beat Leighton to the stick side for a 3-2 lead.

Just 20 seconds later, though, the Flyers tied the score. This time it was Ville Leino who made a pass at the Chicago blue line, hustled to the net and picked up a rebound. Play continued up and down as if the teams wanted to end the game in regulation.

The Flyers held a wide margin in play for the next ten or twelve minutes, but Niemi was rock solid. The Hawks dominated for the last few minutes without getting another goal. Teams headed to overtime for the first time in the series, the Cup more or less hanging in the balance.

One second before the six-minute mark of the fourth period, the Flyers were back in the series. Matt Carle saw Claude Giroux cutting through the slot and made a hard pass. Giroux turned and redirected the puck between Niemi's legs, giving Philadelphia a 3-2 win and bringing the team right back into the series. Chicago still led two games to one, but Game Four was right back at the Wachovia Center.

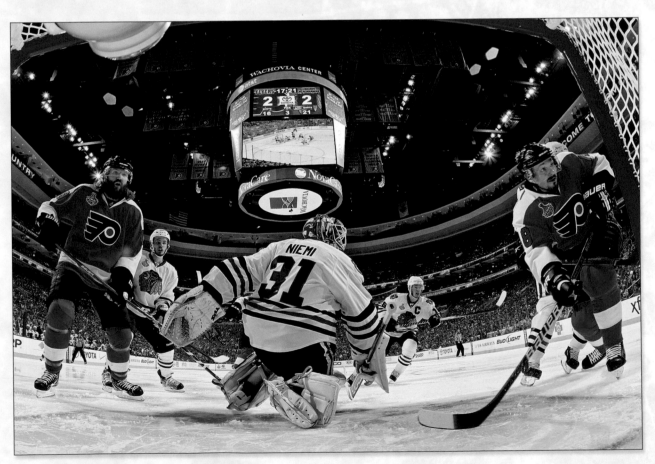

The net cam provides a dramatic shot of Antti Niemi just after making a save, with Flyers pressing his crease looking for a scoring chance.

GAME FOUR — *June 4, 2010*
Chicago 3 at **Philadelphia 5** *(Series tied 2-2)*

At first it looked like a walk in the park for the Flyers. Then it looked like the Hawks would pull off a pretty special rally. But after a Jeff Carter empty-net goal, the Flyers skated off with a 5-3 win in which they dominated for long stretches and fully deserved the victory.

Just like every home game in Philadelphia during the playoffs, it was time for Lauren Hart to sing "God Bless America" in tandem with Kate Smith on the video screen above centre ice.

The duet got the Flyers going right from the opening faceoff, and they had a couple of good scoring chances early before the Hawks got their skates under them and started to press.

The Flyers struck first on a power play. The Hawks won a faceoff deep in their end, and defenceman Niklas Hjalmarsson took the puck around the net casually to start a breakout. But Mike Richards lifted his stick and in the same motion sent a backhander

Chicago's Nick Boynton is stopped in his tracks by Darroll Powe and Blair Betts.

Stanley Cup Final—Chicago Blackhawks vs. Philadelphia Flyers

91

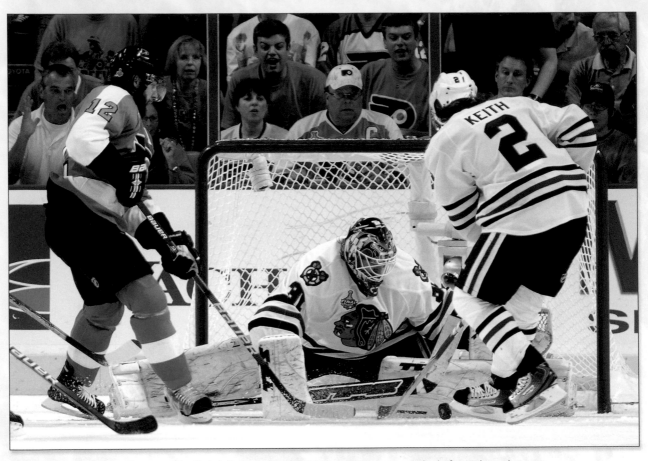

Goalie Antti Niemi makes the save with a little help from Duncan Keith, while Simon Gagne looks for a rebound.

on net, completely surprising goalie Antti Niemi who allowed the puck to slide through his pads.

The Hawks woke up and dominated the next ten minutes of play and more. They were first to the puck, and they established possession in the Philadelphia end and created scoring chances. The only thing they couldn't do was put the puck past Michael Leighton. And then the Flyers had one strong sequence—and scored.

The Hawks failed to clear the puck around the boards, and when it came in front Hjalmarsson whiffed on the puck. It landed on Matt Carle's stick with a half-open net, and he made no mistake. It was the Flyers' first shot since Richards' goal, and it gave Philadelphia a huge 2-0 lead.

Chicago got back into the game at 18:25 when Patrick Sharp tipped a point shot beautifully, but another defensive breakdown gave the Flyers their two-goal lead again. Kimmo Timonen found Claude

Giroux off to the side of the net, and when Niemi came out to challenge him, Timonen just passed it to Niemi's side. Giroux had the empty net, and with 36.3 seconds left in the opening period, it was a crushing goal for the Hawks' chances.

The Flyers stymied the Hawks at every turn in the second period, playing excellent defence without caving in and just sitting on the lead. The scoreless period gave way to a more eventful third, starting with a lucky goal from Ville Leino, whose shot caromed off a stick and floated over Niemi's head and in.

It seemed with a 4-1 lead the Flyers had the game in hand, but Dave Bolland scored on a two-man advantage off a nice pass from Patrick Kane, and then, with just 4:10 remaining, Brian Campbell made it 4-3. The Hawks pressed and pulled Niemi in the final minute, but Duncan Keith bobbled the puck at the blue line allowing Carter to skate in alone on the empty net for the final goal.

Michael Leighton makes a save and has plenty of help to make sure no Blackhawks get to a loose puck.

Stanley Cup Final—Chicago Blackhawks vs. Philadelphia Flyers

93

GAME FIVE — *June 6, 2010*

Philadelphia 4 at **Chicago 7** *(Chicago leads series 3-2)*

In a game similar to the opening game of the series, Chicago scored plenty of goals, chased starting goalie Michael Leighton from the Philadelphia crease, and hung on for a huge win to take control of the quest for the Stanley Cup.

Big Dustin Byfuglien was back with two goals, two assists, and several massive bodychecks. Captain Jonathan Toews and Patrick Kane had their best game of the series, and for the first time the Hawks managed to wear down Flyers' defenceman Chris Pronger.

The pressure was back on the Hawks. They did their job by winning the first two games at home and forcing the Flyers into a desperate situation, but the Flyers responded at home with two wins of their own. In Game Five, a home loss by Chicago would have meant going back to Philadelphia where the Flyers could have closed out the series.

True to form, then, the Hawks dominated the first period by scoring the only three goals and taking it to the Flyers like neither team had done to this point in any previous period. Chicago got an early power play which yielded little, but after eight minutes the Hawks had out-chanced the Flyers 10-0.

Chicago scored first at 12:17 when a quick shot from Kris Versteeg bounced off the leg of Chris Pronger, changed direction, and beat Michael Leighton to the short side. Just three minutes later, it was 2-0 when the Hawks took advantage of a delayed penalty situation. Brent Sopel's point shot just missed the net, but Dave Bolland got the rebound to the side of the net and banked the puck off the back of Leighton's skate and in.

But the Hawks weren't done. They got a goal at 18:15 on a nice play by Versteeg. They came in over

Philadelphia's Mike Richards (left) and Niklas Hjalmarsson go to the corner for a loose puck.

94

Stanley Cup Final—Chicago Blackhawks vs. Philadelphia Flyers

Dustin Byfuglien celebrates a win in Game Five with Patrick Sharp.

the Philadelphia blue line on a three-on-three, but Versteeg criss-crossed with his teammates and let go a quick shot that beat Leighton between the pads. The Hawks went to the dressing room with a huge lead and massive confidence, so now it was a matter of preventing the Flyers from getting back into the game in any way, shape, or form.

It didn't work. The Flyers came out with Brian Boucher in net and looked a lot hungrier and more dangerous. They got on the board just 32 seconds after the faceoff. Ville Leino rammed a bad-angle shot on Niemi, who made the save but lost sight of the puck which squirted past him and lay in the crease. Scott Hartnell was first on the scene and poked the puck into the empty net.

The Flyers caused chaos around Niemi, driving to the net and trying to set up the back-side pass, which they did on several effective occasions. But the Hawks got their three-goal lead back off another unlucky

Pronger deflection. This time it was an Andrew Ladd shot that the Flyers' defenceman blocked. The puck came back to Ladd and he fed Patrick Kane coming down on the left wing. Kane made no mistake, poking the puck in to make it 4-1.

Again, though, the ever-resilient Flyers struck back. In a sequence of complete mayhem around Niemi, the puck drifted into the slot where Kimmo Timonen got off a high shot to make it 4-2.

The Hawks, however, had final say in the period thanks to a great power play. Jonathan Toews came down the left side and fed Byfuglien at the top of the crease, and the big man had only to re-direct the puck between Boucher's pads.

The third period was, if nothing else, wild and unpredictable. The visitors again got the first goal to make it a 5-3 game, thanks to James van Riemsdyk, but Patrick Sharp made a great shot over Boucher's shoulder at 16:08 to make it 6-3 and seemingly salt

Stanley Cup Final—Chicago Blackhawks vs. Philadelphia Flyers

95

away the game. But Duncan Keith broke his stick at the Philadelphia blue line creating a two-on-two the other way, and Leino made a great pass to Simon Gagne who hit an empty net for a 6-4 game.

Coach Peter Laviolette decided to pull Boucher a bit earlier than usual, and the strategy backfired when Byfuglien found the empty net at 17:57. The Hawks proved again they could play with emotion and could score goals, but now they had to return to Philadelphia and try to win the Cup on enemy ice.

"His Airness," Michael Jordan, gets a great reception from the fans during a break in the action.

GAME SIX — *June 9, 2010*

Chicago 4 at Philadelphia 3 (OT)

(Chicago wins Stanley Cup 4-2)

Patrick Kane's goal at 4:06 of overtime gave the Chicago Blackhawks their first Stanley Cup since 1961. It capped an incredible game in which the Hawks twice had leads only to see the Flyers rally late to send the game to a fourth period.

It was the most important game of the season. A Chicago win would give the Blackhawks the Stanley Cup. A Flyers win would send the series to a final game two nights later, in Chicago. So far during these playoffs, the Flyers were 4-0 in games in which they faced elimination—not to mention 9-1 at home in the 2010 post-season. They had experience on their side.

Despite their amazing success at the Wachovia Center, the Flyers were overwhelmed in the opening period, outshot 17-6 by the Hawks and lucky to head the dressing room in a 1-1 tie.

Right from the drop of the puck, the Hawks were the better team, generating chances and maintaining puck possession in the Philadelphia end, showing little of the nerves the Flyers seemed to have.

The Hawks got the first good scoring chance on an early power play when Jonathan Toews hit the post. The puck hopped over his stick on the rebound, and he wasn't able to bat it into an empty net. Moments later, goalie Michael Leighton made a great glove save off another Toews's shot.

Flyers' rookie sensation Ville Leino tries to get off a backhand shot in a crowded crease around goalie Antti Niemi.

Stanley Cup Final —Chicago Blackhawks vs. Philadelphia Flyers

97

Chicago clicked on a later power play when Dustin Byfuglien banged in a puck off a great pass from Toews at 16:49. Before the period ended, though, the Flyers connected on a power play. Scott Hartnell knocked in a loose puck, giving the team and the fans renewed life.

The second period started in spectacular fashion. Seconds after the faceoff, Marian Hossa was stripped of the puck at centre ice and Simon Gagne had a clear breakaway for half the length of the ice. He was bested by a great right-pad save by Niemi.

Unfazed, the Hawks picked up where they left off in the first. Again they were the dominant and hungrier team, creating more offence and playing excellent defence. Everything changed thanks to another horrible error. Ville Leino got a loose puck at the Chicago blue line and Duncan Keith turned to face the play. He fell flat on his behind, though, giving Leino and teammate Daniel Briere a clear path to the goal. Leino fed Briere at the perfect moment, and Briere roofed the puck into the open side of the net at 8:00 to give the Flyers a 2-1 lead.

Two minutes later, Keith atoned for his gaffe and helped tie the game. He got the puck in his own end and rushed up ice with Dave Bolland and Patrick Sharp, creating an odd-man rush on the counter attack. A nice passing play set up Sharp on the right side, and he finished the play with a quick shot that slipped between the pads of Michael Leighton.

With just 2:17 left in the period, the Hawks took the lead again. Kane moved the puck across the point to Niklas Hjalmarsson, and his shot from the top of the

Patrick Sharp looks to the heavens after tying the game, 2-2, in the second period.

circle was perfectly tipped in front by Andrew Ladd. The Hawks held a 26-13 advantage in shots, and a 3-2 lead, with only 20 minutes standing between them and the Stanley Cup.

Alas, it wasn't going to be so easy. Despite playing 15 flawless minutes of defence in the third, the Hawks let the lead slip away with just 3:59 remaining on the clock. Ville Leino made an end-to-end dash and wound up in the corner of Chicago's goal. With little else to do, he tossed the puck in front and it bounced Scott Hartnell's way. Hartnell got enough of his stick on it to poke it to the back side, tying the game 3-3 and sending it to overtime.

That set the stage for Kane's goal, which might well have been the strangest Cup winner of all time. With the Hawks applying tremendous pressure early in overtime, the Flyers managed to gain control of the puck behind their own net. However, they missed an opportunity to move the puck from their zone when Campbell stopped a clearing attempt at the blue line. He passed the puck off to Kane who circled inside the Flyers' zone and let go a quick shot near the end red line. The quick shot beat Leighton between the pads, and the puck settled in the mesh. For for several seconds it seemed that only Kane knew it was in. He raised his arms, tossed his stick and gloves in the air, and raced to the Blackhawks' net. Soon everyone realized that Chicago had won the Cup. Then the celebration began in earnest.

Patrick Kane (far right) reacts after scoring the Stanley Cup-winning goal in overtime as teammates catch up with him to celebrate.

Stanley Cup Final —Chicago Blackhawks vs. Philadelphia Flyers

99

Stanley Cup Final —Chicago Blackhawks vs. Philadelphia Flyers

Captain Jonathan Toews accepts the Cup from NHL Commissioner Gary Bettman.

Marian Hossa is the second player to hoist the Cup as captain Jonathan Toews looks on.

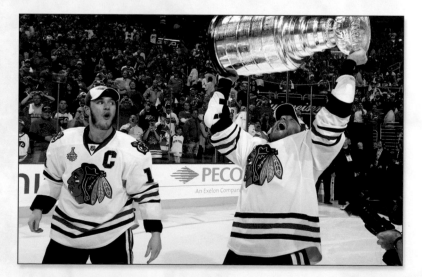

[opposite] Members of the Blackhawks jump their goalie, Antti Niemi, after winning the Stanley Cup in overtime.

Stanley Cup Final —Chicago Blackhawks vs. Philadelphia Flyers

101

Stanley Cup Final — Chicago Blackhawks vs. Philadelphia Flyers

Jonathan Toews receives the Conn Smythe Trophy from NHL Commissioner Gary Bettman in recognition of being the best player in the playoffs.

[opposite] *Defenceman Niklas Hjalmarsson lifts the Cup jubilantly after victory.*

When the Hawks faced Detroit in a best-of-seven for the Stanley Cup in 1961, it marked the team's first appearance in the Final since 1944. They finished in third place in the six-team NHL during the regular season and had the daunting task of playing Montreal in the semi-final.

The Canadiens placed first overall in the standings, 17 points ahead of Chicago. The Habs had also won the Stanley Cup the previous five years in a row, but it was the Hawks who ended Montreal's Cup run by eliminating them in six games. Detroit finished fourth in the standings, but it, too, knocked off the favoured Maple Leafs.

Bill Hay led the team with 61 points and Bobby Hull had 31 goals and 56 points. Incredibly, goalie Glenn Hall played all 70 games and 4,200 minutes for the Hawks in the regular season as well as all 12 games and 772 minutes in the playoffs.

The Final featured a unique set-up in which games alternated between cities. That is, the Stadium in Chicago hosted Games One, Three, and Five of the Final and the Olympia in Detroit was the venue for Games Two, Four, and Six. The home team won each of the first five games, and then in Game Six, in Detroit, the Hawks won the Cup with a 5-1 road victory. It was their last Cup victory before 2010, the longest drought in the NHL. That unfortunate distinction now belongs to the Toronto Maple Leafs, who last won in 1967.

Goalie Glenn Hall hunches over awaiting a faceoff in his end during the 1960-61 season, the last time the Blackhawks won the Stanley Cup.

	GP	W	L	T	GF	GA	Pts		GP	W	L	T	GF	GA	Pts
1926-27	44	19	22	3	115	116	41	1969-70	76	45	22	9	250	170	99
1927-28	44	7	34	3	68	134	17	1970-71	78	49	20	9	277	184	107
1928-29	44	7	29	8	33	85	22	1971-72	78	46	17	15	256	166	107
1929-30	44	21	18	5	117	111	47	1972-73	78	42	27	9	284	225	93
1930-31	44	24	17	3	108	78	51	1973-74	78	41	14	23	272	164	105
1931-32	48	18	19	11	86	101	47	1974-75	80	37	35	8	268	241	82
1932-33	48	16	20	12	88	101	44	1975-76	80	32	30	18	254	261	82
1933-34	48	20	17	11	88	53	51	1976-77	80	26	43	11	240	298	63
1934-35	48	26	17	5	118	88	57	1977-78	80	32	29	19	230	220	83
1935-36	48	21	19	8	93	92	50	1978-79	80	29	36	15	244	277	73
1936-37	48	14	27	7	99	131	35	1979-80	80	34	27	19	241	250	87
1937-38	48	14	25	9	97	139	37	1980-81	80	31	33	16	304	315	78
1938-39	48	12	28	8	91	132	32	1981-82	80	30	38	12	332	363	72
1939-40	48	23	19	6	112	120	52	1982-83	80	47	23	10	338	268	104
1940-41	48	16	25	7	112	139	39	1983-84	80	30	42	8	277	311	68
1941-42	48	22	23	3	145	155	47	1984-85	80	38	35	7	309	299	83
1942-43	50	17	18	15	179	180	49	1985-86	80	39	33	8	351	349	86
1943-44	50	22	23	5	178	187	49	1986-87	80	29	37	14	290	310	72
1944-45	50	13	30	7	141	194	33	1987-88	80	30	41	9	284	328	69
1945-46	50	23	20	7	200	178	53	1988-89	80	27	41	12	297	335	66
1946-47	60	19	37	4	193	274	42	1989-90	80	41	33	6	316	294	88
1947-48	60	20	34	6	195	225	46	1990-91	80	49	23	8	284	211	106
1948-49	60	21	31	8	173	211	50	1991-92	80	36	29	15	257	236	87
1949-50	70	22	38	10	203	244	54	1992-93	84	47	25	12	279	230	106
1950-51	70	13	47	10	171	280	36	1993-94	84	39	36	9	254	240	87
1951-52	70	17	44	9	158	241	43	1994-95	48	24	19	5	156	115	53
1952-53	70	27	28	15	169	175	69	1995-96	82	40	28	14	273	220	94
1953-54	70	12	51	7	133	242	31	1996-97	82	34	35	13	223	210	81
1954-55	70	13	40	17	161	235	43	1997-98	82	30	39	13	193	199	73
1955-56	70	19	39	12	155	216	50	1998-99	82	29	41	12	202	248	70
1956-57	70	16	39	15	169	225	47								
1957-58	70	24	39	7	163	202	55		GP	W	L	OTL	GF	GA	Pts
1958-59	70	28	29	13	197	208	69	1999-2000	82	33	37	10	242	245	78
1959-60	70	28	29	13	191	180	69	2000-01	82	29	40	8	210	246	71
1960-61	70	29	24	17	198	180	75	2001-02	82	41	27	13	216	207	96
1961-62	70	31	26	13	217	186	75	2002-03	82	30	33	13	207	226	79
1962-63	70	32	21	17	194	178	81	2003-04	82	20	43	11	188	259	59
1963-64	70	36	22	12	218	169	84	2004-05	No Season						
1964-65	70	34	28	8	224	176	76	2005-06	82	26	43	13	211	285	65
1965-66	70	37	25	8	240	187	82	2006-07	82	31	42	9	201	258	71
1966-67	70	41	17	12	264	170	94	2007-08	82	40	34	8	239	236	88
1967-68	74	32	26	16	212	222	80	2008-09	82	46	24	12	264	216	104
1968-69	76	34	33	9	280	246	77	2009-10	82	52	22	8	271	209	112

1927

Quarter-final
March 29   Boston 6 at Chicago 1
March 31   Chicago 4 at Boston 4
Boston won total-goals series 10-5

1930

Quarter-final
March 23   Montreal 1 at Chicago 0
March 26   Chicago 2 at Montreal 2 (OT)
Montreal won total-goals series 3-2

1931

Quarter-final
March 24   Chicago 2 at Toronto 2
March 26   Toronto 1 at Chicago 2 (OT)
Chicago won total-goals series 4-3

Semi-final
March 29   NY Rangers 0 at Chicago 2
March 31   Chicago 1 at NY Rangers 0
Chicago won total-goals series 3-0

Final
April 3   Montreal 2 at Chicago 1
April 5   Montreal 1 at Chicago 2 (OT)
April 9   Chicago 3 at Montreal 2 (OT)
April 11   Chicago 2 at Montreal 4
April 14   Chicago 0 at Montreal 2
Montreal won best-of-five 3-2

1932

Quarter-final
March 27   Toronto 0 at Chicago 1
March 29   Chicago 1 at Toronto 6
Toronto won total-goals series 6-2

1934

Quarter-final
March 22   Chicago 3 at Montreal 2
March 25   Montreal 1 at Chicago 1 (OT)
Chicago won total-goals series 4-3

Semi-final
March 28   Chicago 3 at Maroons 0
April 1   Maroons 2 at Chicago 3
Chicago won total-goals series 6-2

Final
April 3   Chicago 2 at Detroit 1 (OT)
April 5   Chicago 4 at Detroit 1
April 8   Detroit 5 at Chicago 2
April 10   Detroit 0 at Chicago 1 (OT)
Chicago won best-of-five 3-1

1935

Quarter-final
March 23   Chicago 0 at Maroons 0
March 26   Maroons 1 at Chicago 0
Maroons won total-goals series 1-0

1936

Quarter-final
March 24   Chicago 0 at NY Americans 3
March 26   NY Americans 4 at Chicago 5
Americans won total-goals series 7-5

1938

Quarter-final
March 22   Chicago 4 at Montreal 6
March 24   Montreal 0 at Chicago 4
March 26   Chicago 3 at Montreal 2 (OT)
Chicago won best-of-three 2-1

Semi-final
March 29   Chicago 1 at NY Americans 3
March 31   NY Americans 0 at Chicago 1 (OT)
April 3   Chicago 3 at NY Americans 2
Chicago won best-of-three 2-1

Final
April 5   Chicago 3 at Toronto 1
April 7   Chicago 1 at Toronto 5
April 10   Toronto 1 at Chicago 2
April 12   Toronto 1 at Chicago 4
Chicago won best-of-five 3-1

1940

Quarter-final
March 19   Chicago 2 at Toronto 3 (OT)
March 21   Toronto 2 at Chicago 1
Toronto won best-of-three 2-0

1941

Quarter-final
March 20   Montreal 1 at Chicago 2
March 22   Chicago 3 at Montreal 4 (OT)
March 25   Montreal 2 at Chicago 3
Chicago won best-of-three 2-1

Semi-final
March 27   Chicago 1 at Detroit 3
March 30   Detroit 2 at Chicago 1 (OT)
Detroit won best-of-three 2-0

1942

Quarter-final
March 22   Boston 2 at Chicago 1 (OT)
March 24   Chicago 4 at Boston 0
March 26   Chicago 2 at Boston 3
Boston won best-of-three 2-1

1944

Semi-final
March 21   Chicago 2 at Detroit 1
March 23   Chicago 1 at Detroit 4
March 26   Detroit 0 at Chicago 2
March 28   Detroit 1 at Chicago 7
March 30   Chicago 5 at Detroit 2
Chicago won best-of-seven 4-1

Final
April 4   Chicago 1 at Montreal 5
April 7   Montreal 3 at Chicago 1
April 9   Montreal 3 at Chicago 2
April 13   Chicago 4 at Montreal 5 (OT)
Montreal won best-of-seven 4-0

1946

Semi-final
March 19   Chicago 2 at Montreal 6
March 21   Chicago 1 at Montreal 5
March 24   Montreal 8 at Chicago 2
March 26   Montreal 7 at Chicago 2
Montreal won best-of-seven 4-0

1953

Semi-final
March 24   Chicago 1 at Montreal 3
March 26   Chicago 3 at Montreal 4
March 29   Montreal 1 at Chicago 2 (OT)
March 31   Montreal 1 at Chicago 3
April 2   Chicago 4 at Montreal 3
April 4   Montreal 3 at Chicago 0
April 7   Chicago 1 at Montreal 4
Montreal won best-of-seven 4-3

1959

Semi-final
March 24   Chicago 2 at Montreal 4
March 26   Chicago 1 at Montreal 5
March 28   Montreal 2 at Chicago 4
March 31   Montreal 1 at Chicago 3
April 2   Chicago 2 at Montreal 4
April 4   Montreal 5 at Chicago 4
Montreal won best-of-seven 4-2

1960

Semi-final
March 24   Chicago 3 at Montreal 4
March 26   Chicago 3 at Montreal 4 (OT)
March 29   Montreal 4 at Chicago 0
March 31   Montreal 2 at Chicago 0
Montreal won best-of-seven 4-0

1961

Semi-final
March 21   Chicago 2 at Montreal 6
March 23   Chicago 4 at Montreal 3
March 26   Montreal 1 at Chicago 2 (OT)
March 28   Montreal 5 at Chicago 2
April 1   Chicago 3 at Montreal 0
April 4   Montreal 0 at Chicago 3
Chicago won best-of-seven 4-2

Final
April 6   Detroit 2 at Chicago 3
April 8   Chicago 1 at Detroit 3
April 10   Detroit 1 at Chicago 3
April 12   Chicago 1 at Detroit 2
April 14   Detroit 3 at Chicago 6
April 16   Chicago 5 at Detroit 1
Chicago won best-of-seven 4-2

1962

Semi-final
March 27   Chicago 1 at Montreal 2
March 29   Chicago 3 at Montreal 4
April 1   Montreal 1 at Chicago 4
April 3   Montreal 3 at Chicago 5
April 5   Chicago 4 at Montreal 3
April 8   Montreal 0 at Chicago 2
Chicago won best-of-seven 4-2

Final
April 10   Chicago 1 at Toronto 4
April 12   Chicago 2 at Toronto 3
April 15   Toronto 0 at Chicago 3
April 17   Toronto 1 at Chicago 4
April 19   Chicago 4 at Toronto 8
April 22   Toronto 2 at Chicago 1
Toronto won best-of-seven 4-2

1963

Semi-final
March 26   Detroit 4 at Chicago 5
March 28   Detroit 2 at Chicago 5
March 31   Chicago 2 at Detroit 4
April 2   Chicago 1 at Detroit 4
April 4   Detroit 4 at Chicago 2
April 7   Chicago 4 at Detroit 7
Detroit won best-of-seven 4-2

1964

Semi-final
March 26   Detroit 1 at Chicago 4
March 29   Detroit 5 at Chicago 4
March 31   Chicago 0 at Detroit 3
April 2   Chicago 3 at Detroit 2 (OT)
April 5   Detroit 2 at Chicago 3
April 7   Chicago 2 at Detroit 7
April 9   Detroit 4 at Chicago 2
Detroit won best-of-seven 4-3

1965

Semi-final
April 1   Chicago 3 at Detroit 4
April 4   Chicago 3 at Detroit 6
April 6   Detroit 2 at Chicago 5
April 8   Detroit 1 at Chicago 2
April 11   Chicago 2 at Detroit 4
April 13   Detroit 0 at Chicago 4
April 15   Chicago 4 at Detroit 2
Chicago won best-of-seven 4-3

Final
April 17   Chicago 2 at Montreal 3
April 20   Chicago 0 at Montreal 2
April 22   Montreal 1 at Chicago 3
April 25   Montreal 1 at Chicago 5
April 27   Chicago 0 at Montreal 6
April 29   Montreal 1 at Chicago 2
May 1   Chicago 0 at Montreal 4
Montreal won best-of-seven 4-3

1966

Semi-final
April 7   Detroit 1 at Chicago 2
April 10   Detroit 7 at Chicago 0
April 12   Chicago 2 at Detroit 1
April 14   Chicago 1 at Detroit 5
April 17   Detroit 5 at Chicago 3
April 19   Chicago 2 at Detroit 3
Detroit won best-of-seven 4-2

1967

Semi-final
April 6   Toronto 2 at Chicago 5
April 9   Toronto 3 at Chicago 1
April 11   Chicago 1 at Toronto 3
April 13   Chicago 4 at Toronto 3
April 15   Toronto 4 at Chicago 2
April 18   Chicago 1 at Toronto 3
Toronto won best-of-seven 4-2

1968

Quarter-final
April 4   Chicago 1 at Rangers 3
April 9   Chicago 1 at Rangers 2
April 11   Rangers 4 at Chicago 7
April 13   Rangers 1 at Chicago 3
April 14   Chicago 2 at Rangers 1
April 16   Rangers 1 at Chicago 4
Chicago won best-of-seven 4-2

Semi-final
April 18   Chicago 2 at Montreal 9
April 20   Chicago 1 at Montreal 4
April 23   Montreal 4 at Chicago 2
April 25   Montreal 1 at Chicago 2
April 28   Chicago 3 at Montreal 4 (OT)
Montreal won best-of-seven 4-1

1970

Quarter-final
April 8   Detroit 2 at Chicago 4
April 9   Detroit 2 at Chicago 4
April 11   Chicago 4 at Detroit 2
April 12   Chicago 4 at Detroit 2
Chicago won best-of-seven 4-0

Semi-final
April 19   Boston 6 at Chicago 3
April 21   Boston 4 at Chicago 1
April 23   Chicago 2 at Boston 5
April 26   Chicago 4 at Boston 5
Boston won best-of-seven 4-0

1971

Quarter-final
April 7   Philadelphia 2 at Chicago 5
April 8   Philadelphia 2 at Chicago 6
April 10   Chicago 3 at Philadelphia 2
April 11   Chicago 6 at Philadelphia 2
Chicago won best-of-seven 4-0

Semi-final
April 18   Rangers 2 at Chicago 1 (OT)
April 20   Rangers 0 at Chicago 3
April 22   Chicago 1 at Rangers 4
April 25   Chicago 7 at Rangers 1
April 27   Rangers 2 at Chicago 3 (OT)
April 29   Chicago 2 at Rangers 3 (OT)
May 2   Rangers 2 at Chicago 4
Chicago won best-of-seven 4-3

Final
May 4   Montreal 1 at Chicago 2 (OT)
May 6   Montreal 3 at Chicago 5
May 9   Chicago 2 at Montreal 4
May 11   Chicago 2 at Montreal 5
May 13   Montreal 0 at Chicago 2
May 16   Chicago 3 at Montreal 4
May 18   Montreal 3 at Chicago 2
Montreal won best-of-seven 4-3

1972

Quarter-final
April 5   Pittsburgh 1 at Chicago 3
April 6   Pittsburgh 2 at Chicago 3
April 8   Chicago 2 at Pittsburgh 0
April 9   Chicago 6 at Pittsburgh 5 (OT)
Chicago won best-of-seven 4-0

Semi-final
April 16   Rangers 3 at Chicago 2
April 18   Rangers 5 at Chicago 3
April 20   Chicago 2 at Rangers 3
April 23   Chicago 2 at Rangers 6
NY Rangers won best-of-seven 4-0

1973

Quarter-final
April 4   St. Louis 1 at Chicago 7
April 5   St. Louis 0 at Chicago 1
April 7   Chicago 5 at St. Louis 2
April 8   Chicago 3 at St. Louis 5
April 10   St. Louis 1 at Chicago 6
Chicago won best-of-seven 4-1

Semi-final
April 12   Rangers 4 at Chicago 1
April 15   Rangers 4 at Chicago 5
April 17   Chicago 2 at Rangers 1
April 19   Chicago 3 at Rangers 1
April 24   Rangers 1 at Chicago 4
Chicago won best-of-seven 4-1

Final
April 29   Chicago 3 at Montreal 8
May 1   Chicago 1 at Montreal 4
May 3   Montreal 4 at Chicago 7
May 6   Montreal 4 at Chicago 0
May 8   Chicago 8 at Montreal 7
May 10   Montreal 6 at Chicago 4
Montreal won best-of-seven 4-2

1974

Quarter-final
April 10   Los Angeles 1 at Chicago 3
April 11   Los Angeles 1 at Chicago 4
April 13   Chicago 1 at Los Angeles 0
April 14   Chicago 1 at Los Angeles 5
April 16   Los Angeles 0 at Chicago 1
Chicago won best-of-seven 4-1

Semi-final
April 18   Chicago 4 at Boston 2
April 21   Chicago 6 at Boston 8
April 23   Boston 3 at Chicago 4 (OT)
April 25   Boston 5 at Chicago 2
April 28   Chicago 2 at Boston 6
April 30   Boston 4 at Chicago 2
Boston won best-of-seven 4-2

1975

Preliminary Round
April 8   Chicago 2 at Boston 8
April 10   Boston 3 at Chicago 4 (OT)
April 11   Chicago 6 at Boston 4
Chicago won best-of-three 2-1

Quarter-final
April 13   Chicago 1 at Buffalo 4
April 15   Chicago 1 at Buffalo 3
April 17   Buffalo 4 at Chicago 5 (OT)
April 20   Buffalo 6 at Chicago 2
April 22   Chicago 1 at Buffalo 3
Buffalo won best-of-seven 4-1

1976

Quarter-final
April 11	Chicago 0 at Montreal 4
April 13	Chicago 1 at Montreal 3
April 15	Montreal 2 at Chicago 1
April 18	Montreal 4 at Chicago 1

Montreal won best-of-seven 4-0

1977

Preliminary Round
| April 10 | Chicago 2 at Islanders 5 |
| April 11 | Islanders 2 at Chicago 1 |

NY Islanders won best-of-three 2-0

1978

Quarter-final
April 17	Chicago 1 at Boston 6
April 19	Chicago 3 at Boston 4 (OT)
April 21	Boston 4 at Chicago 3 (OT)
April 23	Boston 5 at Chicago 2

Boston won best-of-seven 4-0

1979

Quarter-final
April 16	Chicago 2 at Islanders 6
April 18	Chicago 0 at Islanders 1 (OT)
April 20	Islanders 4 at Chicago 0
April 22	Islanders 3 at Chicago 1

NY Islanders won best-of-seven 4-0

1980

Preliminary Round
April 10	St. Louis 2 at Chicago 3 (OT)
April 11	St. Louis 1 at Chicago 5
April 13	Chicago 4 at St. Louis 1

Chicago won best-of-five 3-0

Quarter-final
April 16	Chicago 0 at Buffalo 5
April 17	Chicago 4 at Buffalo 6
April 19	Buffalo 2 at Chicago 1
April 20	Buffalo 3 at Chicago 2

Buffalo won best-of-seven 4-0

1981

Preliminary Round
April 8	Chicago 3 at Calgary 4
April 9	Chicago 2 at Calgary 6
April 11	Calgary 5 at Chicago 4 (OT)

Calgary won best-of-five 3-0

1982

Division Semi-final
April 7	Chicago 3 at Minnesota 2 (OT)
April 8	Chicago 5 at Minnesota 3
April 10	Minnesota 7 at Chicago 1
April 11	Minnesota 2 at Chicago 5

Chicago won best-of-five 3-1

Division Final
April 15	Chicago 5 at St. Louis 4
April 16	Chicago 1 at St. Louis 3
April 18	St. Louis 5 at Chicago 6
April 19	St. Louis 4 at Chicago 7
April 21	Chicago 2 at St. Louis 3 (OT)
April 23	St. Louis 0 at Chicago 2

Chicago won best-of-seven 4-2

Conference Final
April 27	Vancouver 2 at Chicago 1 (OT)
April 29	Vancouver 1 at Chicago 4
May 1	Chicago 3 at Vancouver 4
May 4	Chicago 3 at Vancouver 5
May 6	Vancouver 6 at Chicago 2

Vancouver won best-of-seven 4-2

1983

Division Semi-final
April 6	St. Louis 4 at Chicago 2
April 7	St. Louis 2 at Chicago 7
April 9	Chicago 2 at St. Louis 1
April 10	Chicago 5 at St. Louis 3

Chicago won best-of-five 3-1

Division Final
April 14	Minnesota 2 at Chicago 5
April 15	Minnesota 4 at Chicago 7
April 17	Chicago 1 at Minnesota 5
April 18	Chicago 4 at Minnesota 3 (OT)
April 20	Minnesota 2 at Chicago 5

Chicago won best-of-seven 4-1

Conference Final
April 10	Chicago 4 at Edmonton 8
April 11	Chicago 2 at Edmonton 8
April 13	Edmonton 3 at Chicago 2
April 14	Edmonton 6 at Chicago 3

Edmonton won best-of-seven 4-0

1984

Division Semi-final
April 4	Chicago 3 at Minnesota 1
April 5	Chicago 5 at Minnesota 6
April 7	Minnesota 4 at Chicago 1
April 8	Minnesota 3 at Chicago 4
April 10	Chicago 1 at Minnesota 4

Minnesota won best-of-five 3-2

1985

Division Semi-final
April 10	Detroit 5 at Chicago 9
April 11	Detroit 1 at Chicago 6
April 13	Chicago 8 at Detroit 2

Chicago won best-of-five 3-0

Division Final
April 18	Minnesota 8 at Chicago 5
April 21	Minnesota 2 at Chicago 6
April 23	Chicago 5 at Minnesota 3
April 25	Chicago 7 at Minnesota 6 (OT)
April 28	Minnesota 5 at Chicago 4 (OT)
April 30	Chicago 6 at Minnesota 5 (OT)

Chicago won best-of-seven 4-2

Conference Final
May 4	Chicago 2 at Edmonton 11
May 7	Chicago 3 at Edmonton 7
May 9	Edmonton 2 at Chicago 5
May 12	Edmonton 6 at Chicago 8
May 14	Chicago 5 at Edmonton 10
May 16	Edmonton 8 at Chicago 2

Edmonton won best-of-seven 4-2

1986

Division Semi-final
April 9	Toronto 5 at Chicago 3
April 10	Toronto 6 at Chicago 4
April 12	Chicago 2 at Toronto 7

Toronto won best-of-five 3-0

1987

Division Semi-final
April 8	Chicago 1 at Detroit 3
April 9	Chicago 1 at Detroit 5
April 11	Detroit 4 at Chicago 3 (OT)
April 12	Detroit 3 at Chicago 1

Detroit won best-of-seven 4-0

1988

Division Semi-final
April 6	Chicago 1 at St. Louis 4
April 7	Chicago 2 at St. Louis 3
April 9	St. Louis 3 at Chicago 6
April 10	St. Louis 6 at Chicago 5
April 12	Chicago 3 at St. Louis 5

St. Louis won best-of-seven 4-1

1989

Division Semi-final
April 5	Chicago 2 at Detroit 3
April 6	Chicago 5 at Detroit 4 (OT)
April 8	Detroit 2 at Chicago 4
April 9	Detroit 2 at Chicago 3
April 11	Chicago 4 at Detroit 6
April 13	Detroit 1 at Chicago 7

Chicago won best-of-seven 4-2

Division Final
April 18	Chicago 3 at St. Louis 1
April 20	Chicago 4 at St. Louis 5 (OT)
April 22	St. Louis 2 at Chicago 5
April 24	St. Louis 2 at Chicago 3
April 26	Chicago 4 at St. Louis 2

Chicago won best-of-seven 4-1

Conference Final
May 2	Chicago 0 at Calgary 3
May 4	Chicago 4 at Calgary 2
May 6	Calgary 5 at Chicago 2
May 8	Calgary 2 at Chicago 1 (OT)
May 10	Chicago 1 at Calgary 3

Calgary won best-of-seven 4-1

1990

Division Semi-final
April 4	Minnesota 2 at Chicago 1
April 6	Minnesota 3 at Chicago 5
April 8	Chicago 2 at Minnesota 1
April 10	Chicago 0 at Minnesota 4
April 12	Minnesota 1 at Chicago 5
April 14	Chicago 3 at Minnesota 5
April 16	Minnesota 2 at Chicago 5

Chicago won best-of-seven 4-3

Division Final
April 10	St. Louis 4 at Chicago 3
April 11	St. Louis 3 at Chicago 5
April 13	Chicago 4 at St. Louis 5
April 14	Chicago 3 at St. Louis 2

April 16   St. Louis 2 at Chicago 3
April 30   Chicago 2 at St. Louis 4
April 30   St. Louis 2 at Chicago 8
Chicago won best-of-seven 4-3

Conference Final
May 2   Chicago 2 at Edmonton 5
May 4   Chicago 4 at Edmonton 3
May 6   Edmonton 1 at Chicago 5
May 8   Edmonton 4 at Chicago 2
May 10   Chicago 3 at Edmonton 4
May 12   Edmonton 8 at Chicago 4
Edmonton won best-of-seven 4-2

1991

Division Semi-final
April 4   Minnesota 4 at Chicago 3 (OT)
April 6   Minnesota 2 at Chicago 5
April 8   Chicago 6 at Minnesota 5
April 10   Chicago 1 at Minnesota 3
April 12   Minnesota 6 at Chicago 0
April 14   Chicago 1 at Minnesota 3
Minnesota won best-of-seven 4-2

1992

Division Semi-final
April 18   St. Louis 1 at Chicago 3
April 20   St. Louis 5 at Chicago 3
April 22   Chicago 4 at St. Louis 5 (OT)
April 24   Chicago 5 at St. Louis 3
April 26   St. Louis 6 at Chicago 4
April 28   Chicago 2 at St. Louis 1
Chicago won best-of-seven 4-2

Division Final
May 2   Chicago 2 at Detroit 1
May 4   Chicago 3 at Detroit 1
May 6   Detroit 4 at Chicago 5
May 8   Detroit 0 at Chicago 1
Chicago won best-of-seven 4-0

Conference Final
May 16   Edmonton 2 at Chicago 8
May 18   Edmonton 2 at Chicago 4
May 20   Chicago 4 at Edmonton 3 (OT)
May 22   Chicago 5 at Edmonton 1
Chicago won best-of-seven 4-0

Stanley Cup Final
May 26   Chicago 4 at Pittsburgh 5
May 28   Chicago 1 at Pittsburgh 3
May 30   Pittsburgh 1 at Chicago 0
June 1   Pittsburgh 6 at Chicago 5
Pittsburgh won best-of-seven 4-0

1993

Division Semi-final
April 18   St. Louis 4 at Chicago 3
April 21   St. Louis 2 at Chicago 0
April 23   Chicago 0 at St. Louis 3
April 25   Chicago 3 at St. Louis 4 (OT)
St. Louis won best-of-seven 4-0

1994

Conference Quarter-final
April 18   Chicago 1 at Toronto 5
April 20   Chicago 0 at Toronto 1 (OT)
April 23   Toronto 4 at Chicago 5
April 24   Toronto 3 at Chicago 4 (OT)
April 26   Chicago 0 at Toronto 1
April 28   Toronto 1 at Chicago 0
Toronto won best-of-seven 4-2

1995

Conference Quarter-final
May 7   Toronto 5 at Chicago 3
May 9   Toronto 3 at Chicago 0
May 11   Chicago 3 at Toronto 2
May 13   Chicago 3 at Toronto 1
May 15   Toronto 2 at Chicago 4
May 17   Chicago 4 at Toronto 5 (OT)
May 19   Toronto 1 at Chicago 5
Chicago won best-of-seven 4-3

Conference Semi-final
May 21   Vancouver 1 at Chicago 2 (OT)
May 23   Vancouver 0 at Chicago 2
May 25   Chicago 3 at Vancouver 2 (OT)
May 27   Chicago 4 at Vancouver 3 (OT)
Chicago won best-of-seven 4-0

Conference Final
June 1   Chicago 1 at Detroit 2 (OT)
June 4   Chicago 2 at Detroit 3
June 6   Detroit 4 at Chicago 3 (OT)
June 8   Detroit 2 at Chicago 5
June 11   Chicago 1 at Detroit 2 (OT)
Detroit won best-of-seven 4-1

1996

Conference Quarter-final
April 17   Calgary 1 at Chicago 4
April 19   Calgary 0 at Chicago 3
April 21   Chicago 7 at Calgary 5
April 23   Chicago 2 at Calgary 1 (OT)
Chicago won best-of-seven 4-0

Conference Semi-final
May 2   Chicago 3 at Colorado 2 (OT)
May 4   Chicago 1 at Colorado 5
May 6   Colorado 3 at Chicago 4 (OT)
May 8   Colorado 3 at Chicago 2 (OT)
May 11   Chicago 1 at Colorado 4
May 13   Colorado 4 at Chicago 3 (OT)
Colorado won best-of-seven 4-2

1997

Conference Quarter-final
April 16   Chicago 0 at Colorado 6
April 18   Chicago 1 at Colorado 3
April 20   Colorado 3 at Chicago 4 (OT)
April 22   Colorado 3 at Chicago 6
April 24   Chicago 0 at Colorado 7
April 26   Colorado 6 at Chicago 3
Colorado won best-of-seven 4-2

2002

Conference Quarter-final
April 18   Chicago 2 at St. Louis 1
April 20   Chicago 0 at St. Louis 2
April 21   St. Louis 4 at Chicago 0
April 23   St. Louis 1 at Chicago 0
April 25   Chicago 3 at St. Louis 5
St. Louis won best-of-seven 4-1

(l to r) Tony Esposito, Pierre Pilote, Bobby Hull, Denis Savard, and Stan Mikita, all members of the Hockey Hall of Fame.

BLACKHAWKS IN THE HOCKEY HALL OF FAME

Players

Sid Abel (1969)
Doug Bentley (1964)
Max Bentley (1966)
George Boucher (1960)
Frank Brimsek (1966)
Billy Burch (1974)
Lionel Conacher (1994)
Roy Conacher (1998)
Art Coulter (1974)
Babe Dye (1970)
Tony Esposito (1988)
Phil Esposito (1984)
Bill Gadsby (1970)
Charlie Gardiner (1945)
Michel Goulet (1998)
Glenn Hall (1975)
George Hay (1958)
Bobby Hull (1983)

Dick Irvin (1958)
Duke Keats (1958)
Hugh Lehman (1958)
Ted Lindsay (1966)
Harry Lumley (1980)
Duncan MacKay (1952)
Stan Mikita (1983)
Howie Morenz (1945)
Bill Mosienko (1965)
Bert Olmstead (1985)
Bobby Orr (1979)
Pierre Pilote (1975)
Denis Savard (2000)
Earl Siebert (1963)
Clint Smith (1991)
Allan Stanley (1981)
John Stewart (1964)
Harry Watson (1994)

Builders

Al Arbour (1996)
Tommy Ivan (1974)
John Mariucci (1985)
Fred McLaughlin (1963)
Jim D. Norris (1962)
Jim Norris (1958)
Rudy Pilous (1985)
Bud Poile (1990)
Art Wirtz (1971)
Bill Wirtz (1976)

RETIRED NUMBERS

Retired Numbers

1	**Glenn Hall**	November 20, 1998
3	**Pierre Pilote**	November 12, 2008
3	**Keith Magnuson**	November 12, 2008
3	**Bobby Hull**	December 18, 1993
18	**Denis Savard**	March 19, 1998
21	**Stan Mikita**	October 19, 1980
35	**Tony Esposito**	November 20, 1998

Stan Mikta addresses the crowd on March 7, 2008, during a ceremony to honour both him (#21) and Bobby Hull (#9, behind, smiling).

Jack Adams Award

1983	Orval Tessier

Hart Memorial Trophy

1946	Max Bentley
1954	Al Rollins
1965	Bobby Hull
1966	Bobby Hull
1967	Stan Mikita
1968	Stan Mikita

Art Ross Trophy

1943	Doug Bentley
1946	Max Bentley
1947	Max Bentley
1949	Roy Conacher
1960	Bobby Hull
1962	Bobby Hull
1964	Stan Mikita
1965	Stan Mikita
1966	Bobby Hull
1967	Stan Mikita
1968	Stan Mikita

James Norris Memorial Trophy

1963	Pierre Pilote
1964	Pierre Pilote
1965	Pierre Pilote

Frank J. Selke Trophy

1986	Troy Murray
1991	Dirk Graham

Calder Memorial Trophy

1936	Mike Karakas
1938	Carl Dahlstrom
1955	Ed Litzenberger
1960	Bill Hay
1970	Tony Esposito
1983	Steve Larmer
1991	Ed Belfour
2008	Patrick Kane

Lady Byng Memorial Trophy

1936	Doc Romnes
1943	Max Bentley
1944	Clint Smith
1945	Bill Mosienko
1964	Ken Wharram
1965	Bobby Hull
1967	Stan Mikita
1968	Stan Mikita

Vezina Trophy

1932	Chuck Gardiner
1934	Chuck Gardiner
1935	Lorne Chabot
1963	Glenn Hall
1967	Glenn Hall/Dennis DeJordy
1970	Tony Esposito
1972	Tony Esposito/ Gary Smith
1974	Tony Esposito (& Bernie Parent, Philadelphia)
1991	Ed Belfour
1993	Ed Belfour

William M. Jennings Trophy

1991	Ed Belfour
1993	Ed Belfour/Jimmy Waite
1995	Ed Belfour

Bill Masterton Memorial Trophy

1970	Pit Martin
2004	Bryan Berard

Lester Patrick Trophy

1967	James Norris
1969	Bobby Hull
1972	James D. Norris
1975	Tommy Ivan
1976	Stan Mikita
1978	Bill Wirtz
1985	Art Wirtz

Goalie Tony Esposito.

2009

28	Dylan Olsen
59	Brandon Pirri
89	Daniel Delisle
119	Byron Froese
149	Marcus Kruger
177	David Pacan
195	Paul Phillips
209	David Gilbert

2008

11	Kyle Beach
68	Shawn Lalonde
132	Teigan Zahn
162	Jonathan Carlsson
169	Ben Smith
179	Braden Birch
192	Joe Gleason

2007

1	Patrick Kane
38	Billy Sweatt
56	Akim Aliu
69	Maxime Tanguay
86	Josh Unice
126	Joe Lavin
156	Richard Greenop

2006

3	Jonathan Toews
33	Igor Makarov
61	Simon Danis-Pepin
76	Tony Lagerstrom
95	Ben Shutron
96	Joe Palmer
156	Jan-Mikael Jutilainen
169	Chris Auger
186	Peter Leblanc

2005

7	Jack Skille
43	Mike Blunden
54	Dan Bertram
68	Evan Brophey
108	Niklas Hjalmarsson
113	Nathan Davis
117	Denis Istomin
134	Brennan Turner
167	Joe Fallon
188	Joe Charlebois
202	David Kuchejda
203	Adam Hobson

2004

3	Cam Barker
32	Dave Bolland
41	Bryan Bickell
45	Ryan Garlock
54	Jakub Sindel
68	Adam Berti
120	Mitch Maunu
123	Karel Hromas
131	Trevor Kell
140	Jake Dowell
165	Scott McCulloch
196	Petri Kontiola

214	Troy Brouwer
223	Jared Walker
229	Eric Hunter
256	Matthew Ford
260	Marko Anttila

2003

14	Brent Seabrook
52	Corey Crawford
59	Michal Barinka
151	Lasse Kukkonen
156	Alexei Ivanov
181	Johan Andersson
211	Mike Brodeur
245	Dustin Byfuglien
275	Michael Grenzy
282	Chris Porter

2002

21	Anton Babchuk
54	Duncan Keith
93	Alexander Kozhevnikov
128	Matt Ellison
156	James Wisniewski
188	Kevin Kantee
219	Tyson Kellerman
251	Jason Kostadine
282	Adam Burish

2001

9	Tuomo Ruutu
29	Adam Munro
59	Matt Keith
73	Craig Anderson
104	Brent MacLellan
115	Vladimir Gusev
119	Alexei Zotkin
142	Tommi Jaminki
174	Alexander Golovin
186	Petr Puncochar
205	Teemu Jaaskelainen
216	Oleg Minakov
268	Jeff Miles

2000

10	Mikhail Yakubov
11	Pavel Vorobiev
49	Jonas Nordqvist
74	Igor Radulov
106	Scotty Balan
117	Olli Malmivaara
151	Alexander Barkunov
177	Mike Ayers
193	Joey Martin
207	Cliff Loya
225	Vladislav Luchkin
240	Adam Berkhoel
262	Peter Flache
271	Reto Von Arx
291	Arne Ramholt

1999

23	Steve McCarthy
46	Dmitri Levinsky
63	Stepan Mokhov
134	Michael Jacobsen

165	Mike Leighton
194	Mattias Wennerberg
195	Yorick Treille
223	Andrew Carver

1998

8	Mark Bell
94	Matthias Trattnig
156	Kent Huskins
158	Jari Viuhkola
166	Jonathan Pelletier
183	Tyler Arnason
210	Sean Griffin
238	Alexandre Couture
240	Andrei Yershov

1997

13	Daniel Cleary
16	Ty Jones
39	Jeremy Reich
67	Mike Souza
110	Ben Simon
120	Pete Gardiner
130	Kyle Calder
147	Heath Gordon
174	Jared Smith
204	Sergei Shikhanov
230	Chris Feil

1996

31	Remi Royer
42	Jeff Paul
46	Geoff Peters
130	Andy Johnson
184	Mike Vellinga
210	Chris Twerdun
236	Andrei Kozyrev

1995

19	Dmitri Nabokov
45	Christian Laflamme
71	Kevin McKay
82	Chris Van Dyk
97	Pavel Kriz
146	Marc Magliarditi
149	Marty Wilford
175	Steve Tardif
201	Casey Hankinson
227	Michael Pittman

1994

14	Ethan Moreau
40	Jean-Yves Leroux
85	Steve McLaren
118	Marc Dupuis
144	Jim Ensom
170	Tyler Prosofsky
196	Mike Josephson
222	Lubomir Jandera
248	Lars Weibel
263	Rob Mara

1993

24	Eric Lecompte
50	Eric Manlow
54	Bogdan Savenko

76	Ryan Huska
90	Eric Daze
102	Patrick Pysz
128	Jonni Vauhkonen
180	Tom White
206	Sergei Petrov
232	Mike Rusk
258	Mike McGhan
284	Tom Noble

1992

12	Sergei Krivokrasov
36	Jeff Shantz
41	Sergei Klimovich
89	Andy MacIntyre
113	Tim Hogan
137	Gerry Skrypec
161	Mike Prokopec
185	Layne Roland
209	David Hymovitz
233	Richard Raymond

1991

22	Dean McAmmond
39	Mike Pomichter
44	Jamie Matthews
66	Bobby House
71	Igor Kravchuk
88	Zac Boyer
110	Maco Balkovec
112	Kevin St. Jacques
132	Jacques Auger
154	Scott Kirton
176	Roch Belley
198	Scott MacDonald
220	Alexander Andrijevski
242	Mike Larkin
264	Scott Dean

1990

16	Karl Dykhuis
37	Ivan Droppa
79	Chris Tucker
121	Brent Stickney
124	Derek Edgerly
163	Hugo Belanger
184	Owen Lessard
205	Erik Peterson
226	Steve Dubinsky
247	Dino Grossi

1989

6	Adam Bennett
27	Mike Speer
48	Bob Kellogg
111	Tommi Pullola
132	Tracy Egeland
153	Milan Tichy
174	Jason Greyerbiehl
195	Matt Saunders
216	Mike Kozak
237	Mike Doneghey

1988

8	Jeremy Roenick
50	Trevor Dam

71	Stefan Elvenes					109	Wayne Dye
92	Joe Cleary					125	Jim Koleff
113	Justin Lafayette					140	Jack Johnson
134	Craig Woodcroft					141	Steve Alley
155	Jon Pojar					156	Rick Clubbe
176	Matt Hentges					165	Gene Strate
197	Daniel Maurice						
218	Dirk Tenzer						
239	Andreas Lupzig						

1983

18	Bruce Cassidy
39	Wayne Presley
59	Marc Bergevin
79	Tarek Howard
99	Kevin Robinson
115	Jari Torkki
119	Mark LaVarre
139	Scott Birnie
159	Kent Paynter
179	Brian Noonan
199	Dominik Hasek
219	Steve Pepin

1978

10	Tim Higgins
29	Doug Lecuyer
46	Rick Paterson
63	Brian Young
79	Mark Murphy
96	Dave Feamster
113	Dave Mancuso
130	Sandy Ross
147	Mark Locken
164	Glenn Van
179	Darryl Sutter

1972

13	Phil Russell
29	Brian Ogilvie
45	Mike Veisor
61	Tom Peluso
77	Rejean Giroux
93	Rob Palmer
109	Terry Smith
125	Billy Reay
141	Gary Donaldson

1987

8	Jimmy Waite
29	Ryan McGill
50	Cam Russell
60	Mike Dagenais
92	Ulf Sandstrom
113	Mike McCormick
134	Stephen Tepper
155	John Reilly
176	Lance Werness
197	Dale Marquette
218	Bill LaCouture
239	Mike Lappin

1982

7	Ken Yaremchuk
28	Rene Badeau
49	Tom McMurchy
70	Bill Watson
91	Brad Beck
112	Mark Hatcher
133	Jay Ness
154	Jeff Smith
175	Phil Patterson
196	Jim Camazzola
217	Mike James
238	Bob Andrea

1977

6	Doug Wilson
19	Jean Savard
60	Randy Ireland
78	Gary Platt
96	Jack O'Callahan
114	Floyd Lahache
129	Jeff Geiger
144	Steve Ough

1971

12	Dan Spring
26	Dave Kryskow
40	Bob Peppler
54	Clyde Simon
68	Dean Blais
82	Jim Johnston

1986

14	Everett Sanipass
35	Mark Kurzawski
77	Frantisek Kucera
98	Lonnie Loach
119	Mario Doyon
140	Mike Hudson
161	Marty Nanne
182	Geoff Benic
203	Glenn Lowes
224	Chris Thayer
245	Sean Williams

1981

12	Tony Tanti
25	Kevin Griffin
54	Darrell Anholt
75	Perry Pelensky
96	Doug Chessell
117	Bill Schafhauser
138	Marc Centrone
159	Johan Mellstron
180	John Benns
201	Sylvain Roy

1976

9	Real Cloutier
27	Jeff McDill
45	Thomas Gradin
63	Dave Debol
81	Terry McDonald
99	John Peterson
115	John Rothstein

1970

14	Dan Maloney
28	Michel Archambault
42	Len Frig
56	Walt Ledingham
70	Gilles Meloche

1985

11	Dave Manson
53	Andy Helmuth
74	Dan Vincelette
87	Rick Herbert
95	Brad Belland
116	Jonas Heed
137	Victor Posa
158	John Reid
179	Richard Laplante
200	Brad Hamilton
221	Ian Pound
242	Richard Braccia

1980

3	Denis Savard
15	Jerry Dupont
28	Steve Ludzik
30	Ken Solheim
36	Len Dawes
57	Troy Murray
58	Marcel Frere
67	Carey Wilson
78	Brian Shaw
99	Kevin Ginnell
120	Steve Larmer
141	Sean Simpson
162	Jim Ralph
183	Don Dietrich
204	Dan Frawley

1975

7	Greg Vaydik
25	Danny Arndt
43	Mike O'Connell
61	Pierre Giroux
79	Bob Hoffmeyer
97	Tom Ulseth
115	Ted Bulley
133	Paul Jensen

1969

13	J.P. Bordeleau
24	Larry Romanchych
36	Milt Black
48	Darryl Maggs
60	Mike Baumgartner
71	Dave Hudson

1968

9	John Marks

1984

3	Ed Olczyk
45	Trent Yawney
66	Tom Eriksson
90	Timo Lehkonen
101	Darin Sceviour
111	Chris Clifford
132	Mike Stapleton
153	Glenn Greenough
174	Ralph DiFiori
194	Joakim Persson
215	Bill Brown
224	David Mackey
235	Dan Williams

1979

7	Keith Brown
28	Tim Trimper
49	Bill Gardner
70	Louis Begin
91	Lowell Loveday
112	Doug Crossman

1974

16	Grant Mulvey
34	Alain Daigle
52	Bob Murray
70	Terry Ruskowski
88	Dave Logan
106	Bob Volpe
124	Eddie Mio
141	Mike St. Cyr
158	Steve Colp
173	Rick Fraser
188	Jean Bernier
200	Dwayne Byers
210	Glen Ing

1967

7	Bob Tombari

1966

3	Terry Caffery
9	Ron Dussiaume
15	Larry Gibbons
21	Brian Morenz

1965

2	Andy Culligan
7	Brian McKenney

1973

13	Darcy Rota
29	Reg Thomas
45	Randy Holt
61	Dave Elliott
77	Dan Hinton
93	Garry Doerksen

1964

4	Richie Bayes
10	Jan Popiel
16	Carl Hadfield
22	Moe L'Abbe

1963

5	Art Hampson
11	Wayne Davison
16	Bill Carson

Bickell, Bryan

b. Bowmanville, Ontario, March 9, 1986

Left wing—shoots left

6'4" 223 lbs.

Drafted 41st overall by Chicago in 2004

Part of the young corps of the team, Bickell signed his first contract (a three-year deal) with Chicago in 2006 after four years in the OHL with Ottawa 67's and Windsor Spitfires. Big and tough, offence is not his forte so much as physical play on the fourth line.

Bickell started the 2006-07 season in the AHL with Norfolk, but was called up to the Hawks on April 5, 2007. He scored a goal in his NHL debut, a 3-2 win over Detroit, but he has been a minor leaguer most of the time since, in Rockford of the AHL. He has been recalled more than a dozen times, sometimes not dressing, other times getting in a few games, and he was used by coach Joel Quenneville as insurance during the 2010 playoffs.

Although he re-signed with the team last summer, he will be a free agent in July 2010.

Career Statistics		Regular Season					Playoffs				
		GP	G	A	P	Pim	GP	G	A	P	Pim
2006-07	CHI	9	0	0	0	2	DNQ				
2007-08	CHI	81	4	4	8	214	DNQ				
2008-09	CHI	66	6	3	9	93	17	3	2	5	30
2009-10	CHI	13	1	3	4	14	FOR 2010 PLAYOFF STATS SEE P. 28				
Totals		169	11	10	21	323					

Bolland, Dave

b. Mimico, Ontario, June 5, 1986

Centre—shoots right

6' 181 lbs.

Drafted 32nd overall by Chicago in 2004

Just 23 years old when the 2010 Stanley Cup Final began, Bolland has tremendous upside, as the scouts like to say. He had an excellent junior career that included four years with the OHL's London Knights, culminating in his final season, 2005-06.

That year, Bolland led the OHL with 57 goals and was second in points with 130 behind teammate Robbie Schremp. In January 2006, he helped Canada win gold at the World Junior Championship (with teammate Jonathan Toews). The previous year he took the Knights to the Memorial Cup, leading the playoffs with 15 goals in as many games.

Bolland played most of his first two years of pro with Norfolk, Chicago's AHL affiliate. He appeared in his first NHL game on October 25, 2006, and the next year he played in 39 games. In 2008, he finally made the Hawks out of training camp, recording an impressive 19 goals.

Unfortunately, Bolland wasn't able to build off this fine rookie season. Midway through 2009-10 he required back surgery and missed 41 games, although he did return to provide some offence and solid two-way play in the post-season.

Career Statistics		Regular Season					Playoffs				
		GP	G	A	P	Pim	GP	G	A	P	Pim
2006-07	CHI	1	0	0	0	0	DNQ				
2007-08	CHI	39	4	13	17	28	DNQ				
2008-09	CHI	81	19	28	47	52	17	4	8	12	24
2009-10	CHI	39	6	10	16	28	FOR 2010 PLAYOFF STATS SEE P. 28				
Totals		160	29	51	80	108					

Brouwer, Troy

b. Vancouver, British Columbia,
August 17, 1985

Right wing—shoots right

6'2" 213 lbs.

Drafted 214th overall by Chicago in 2004

Like so many other players on this young Hawks'
team, Troy Brouwer has developed ahead of schedule
and expectations. He was Chicago's 13th draft choice
in 2004 after completing his second of what would be
five seasons junior hockey with Moose Jaw Warriors in
the WHL. It was in his final year of junior, as an over-
age player, that he started to show potential. That year
he was team captain and led the WHL with 102 points,
the only player to reach the century mark.

Brouwer turned pro in the summer of 2006 and
over the course of the next three years developed into
a solid if unspectacular player. He played more with
the Hawks and less with the AHL affiliate in Norfolk
and Rockford, learning to score at the higher levels as
he had in junior.

In his first full season with Chicago, Brouwer had
ten goals, but this past season he increased that to 22.
His play in the post-season was also impressive, and
his two goals in the opening game of the finals against
Philadelphia contributed to the team's 6-5 win.

The key to Brouwer's success lies in his style of
play. He has the shot and hands of a goalscorer but
the temperament sometimes of a fighter. A true power
forward, he is at his best when he uses his size and
strength to generate scoring chances rather than
merely to overpower or intimidate the opposition.
Only 24 years old and with a Stanley Cup under his
belt, the future looks great for Brouwer.

Career Statistics		Regular Season					Playoffs				
		GP	G	A	P	Pim	GP	G	A	P	Pim
2006-07	CHI	10	0	0	0	7	DNQ				
2007-08	CHI	2	0	1	1	0	DNQ				
2008-09	CHI	69	10	16	26	50	17	0	2	2	12
2009-10	CHI	78	22	18	40	66	FOR 2010 PLAYOFF STATS SEE P. 28				
Totals		159	32	35	67	123					

Burish, Adam

b. Madison, Wisconsin, January 6, 1983

Right wing—shoots right

6'1" 200 lbs.

Drafted 282nd overall by Chicago in 2002

One of the lowest selections from the 2002 Entry Draft to make it to the NHL, Burish has overcome adversity of all forms to make it to the big league at age 23. When he was in his teens, he was in a serious car accident and missed several months recovering from his injuries.

After being drafted, he attended the University of Wisconsin, staying with the Badgers for the full four years. His NCAA career culminated in 2006 when he captained the team to a championship. Burish assisted on both goals in a 2-1 win.

After spending most of his first pro season in the AHL with Norfolk, Burish made the Hawks full-time in 2007 as a fourth-liner and enforcer. He ranked third in penalty minutes in the NHL that season and established himself as a tough guy to be respected, a player who stood up for his teammates. He was a good skater as well, and was named to Team USA for the 2008 World Championship after the Hawks failed to qualify for the playoffs. This marked his first international experience, and he managed three assists in seven games.

Burish's participation in the 2010 playoffs is exceptional. During the exhibition season he suffered a serious tear of his ACL and missed most of the regular season, returning only for the final 13 games.

Career Statistics		Regular Season					Playoffs				
		GP	G	A	P	Pim	GP	G	A	P	Pim
2006-07	CHI	9	0	0	0	2	DNQ				
2007-08	CHI	81	4	4	8	214	DNQ				
2008-09	CHI	66	6	3	9	93	17	3	2	5	30
2009-10	CHI	13	1	3	4	14	FOR 2010 PLAYOFF STATS SEE P. 28				
Totals		169	11	10	21	323					

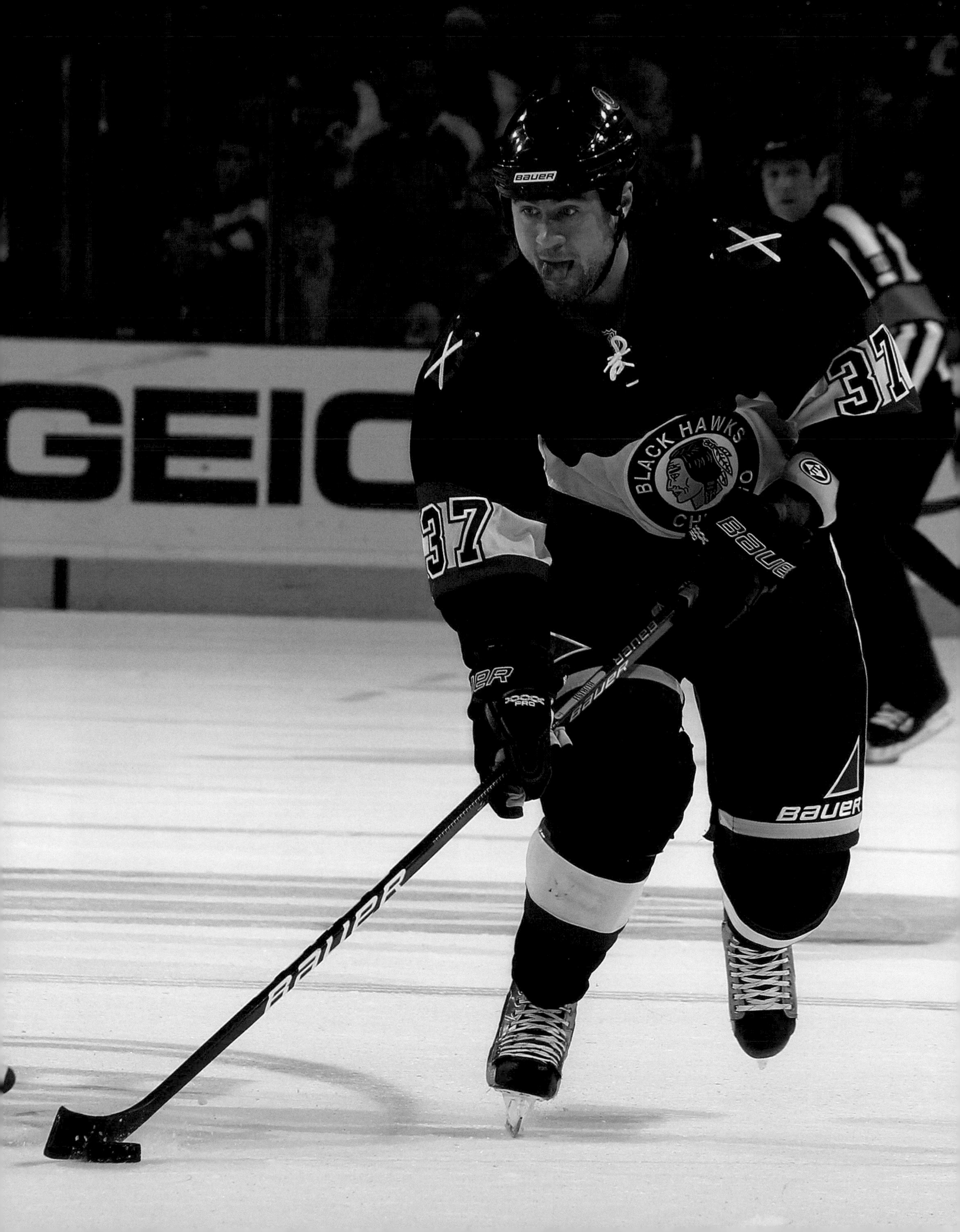
GEIC
BLACK HAWKS
37
BAUER

Byfuglien, Dustin

b. Minneapolis, Minnesota,
March 27, 1985

Left wing—shoots right

6'4" 257 lbs.

Drafted 245th overall by Chicago in 2003

Perhaps more than any other NHL player, Dustin Byfuglien is well-known first and foremost for the unique spelling and pronunciation of his surname. However, "Buff-linn," (the correct pronunciation) is one of the great success stories of the Hawks' current roster.

For starters, he was drafted a lowly 245th overall, a sign to most players they will not make the NHL. Second, Byfuglien started his career as a defenceman in the WHL, but in 2007, his third year with the Hawks, he was moved to right wing to take advantage of his colossal frame. There are not many 246-pound NHLers, and Byfuglien's size alone was intimidating.

Because he is a big man, it took him a bit longer to develop. He split his first three pro seasons between the Hawks and the AHL's Norfolk Admirals. He made his NHL debut on March 1, 2006, scoring the first goal—and game winner—in a 3-0 win over Nashville.

In 2008, Byfuglien finally made the NHL for good. He had 19 goals as a rookie and used his imposing size to good advantage, but it wasn't until the 2010 playoffs that he really distinguished himself on ice and with the fans.

Of his 55 career regular-season goals to date, 12 have been game winners, and his sense of timing and getting the big goal was never more evident than the conference finals against San Jose, a four-game sweep for the Hawks that took them to a Cup showdown with Philadelphia.

Byfuglien scored an amazing three game-winners in the series, the most dramatic in the back-breaking third game at 12:24 of overtime to more or less sink the Sharks. Now 25 years old and approaching his prime, the sky is the limit for the giant with soft hands and a penchant for the dramatic.

Career Statistics		Regular Season				
		GP	G	A	P	Pim
2005-06	CHI	25	3	2	5	24
2006-07	CHI	9	1	2	3	10
2007-08	CHI	67	19	17	36	59
2008-09	CHI	77	15	16	31	81
2009-10	CHI	82	17	17	34	94
Totals		260	55	54	109	268

Playoffs				
GP	G	A	P	Pim
DNQ				
DNQ				
DNQ				
17	3	6	9	26
FOR 2010 PLAYOFF STATS SEE P. 28				

Campbell, Brian

b. Strathroy, Ontario, May 23, 1979

Defence—shoots left

6' 189 lbs.

Drafted 156th overall by Buffalo in 1997

A smooth skater in the tradition of Bobby Orr and Paul Coffey, Brian Campbell had an outstanding junior career before making it to the NHL. He was drafted a lowly 156th overall by Buffalo, but this was after only one season with the Ottawa 67's in the OHL. He went on to develop into a rushing defenceman, culminating in the 1998-99 season when he received several honours.

First, he played for Team Canada at the 1999 World Junior Championship, winning a silver medal. Later, he was named the player of the year in Canadian junior hockey and was named the MVP of the Ontario league.

Campbell split the next three years between the Sabres and the team's AHL affiliate in Rochester, making the team in 2002 as a 23-year-old and never looking back. In the summer of 2008 he was destined to become an unrestricted free agent, and the Sabres, not sure they could re-sign him over the summer, traded him to San Jose prior to the deadline.

After the Sharks were eliminated in the second round of the 2008 playoffs, Campbell exercised his right and tested free agency. He settled on the Hawks not because of the money (although an 8-year, $56-million contract was nothing to sneeze at) but because he believed the Hawks would be a Cup-contending team in the immediate future and for many years to come.

Campbell has averaged more than 22 minutes of ice time a game and has been a vital element of the team's power play. He missed the last 14 games of the regular season after suffering a broken clavicle and broken rib following a hit by Alexander Ovechkin. The injury snapped a 388-game Iron Man streak, but Campbell returned during the first round of the playoffs.

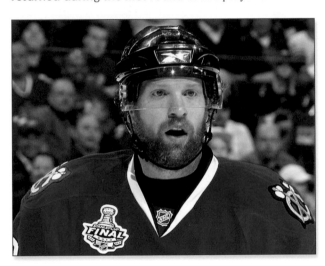

Career Statistics		Regular Season					Playoffs				
		GP	G	A	P	Pim	GP	G	A	P	Pim
1999-00	BUF	12	1	4	5	4	DNP				
2000-01	BUF	8	0	0	0	2	DNP				
2001-02	BUF	29	3	3	6	12	DNQ				
2002-03	BUF	65	2	17	19	20	DNQ				
2003-04	BUF	53	3	8	11	12	DNQ				
2005-06	BUF	79	12	32	44	16	18	0	6	6	12
2006-07	BUF	82	6	42	48	35	16	3	4	7	14
2007-08	BUF	63	5	38	43	12	--	--	--	--	--
2007-08	SJ	20	3	16	19	8	13	1	6	7	4
2008-09	CHI	82	7	45	52	22	17	2	8	10	0
2009-10	CHI	68	7	31	38	18	FOR 2010 PLAYOFF STATS SEE P. 28				
Totals		561	49	236	285	161					

FOR 2010 PLAYOFF STATS SEE P. 28

Eager, Ben

b. Ottawa, Ontario, January 22, 1984

Left wing—shoots left

6'2" 220 lbs.

Drafted 23rd overall by Phoenix in 2002

One of several players in the 2010 Stanley Cup Final who has played for both the Flyers and Hawks, Ben Eager is known more for his fists than his scoring. In four seasons of junior hockey with the Oshawa Generals, he accrued nearly 800 penalty minutes, and he continued his fighting ways in the AHL before making it to the NHL.

Eager led the league in penalty minutes in 2006-07, his first full season in the NHL, although he missed 19 games, and also played briefly in the minors. He was traded to the Hawks on December 18, 2007, for Jim Vandermeer, but soon after joining Chicago he suffered a season-ending shoulder injury.

Slowly but surely he has reduced the fighting aspect of his game, picking and choosing when to establish toughness in favour of more playing time. Although he led the 2009 playoffs in penalty minutes, he had a career season in 2009-10 with 16 scoring points.

Career Statistics		Regular Season					Playoffs				
		GP	G	A	P	Pim	GP	G	A	P	Pim
2005-06	PHI	25	3	5	8	18	DNP				
2006-07	PHI	63	6	5	11	233	DNQ				
2007-08	PHI	23	0	0	0	62	--	--	--	--	--
2007-08	CHI	9	0	2	2	27	DNQ				
2008-09	CHI	75	11	4	15	161	17	1	1	2	61
2009-10	CHI	60	7	9	16	120	FOR 2010 PLAYOFF STATS SEE P. 28				
Totals		255	27	25	52	621					

FOR 2010 PLAYOFF STATS SEE P. 28

Fraser, Colin

b. Sicamous, British Columbia,
January 28, 1985

Centre—shoots left

6'1" 190 lbs.

Drafted 69th overall by Philadelphia in 2003

Although Fraser was drafted in the third round of the Entry Draft by the Flyers seven years ago, he never played with the team. Indeed, he was part of a multi-player deal which saw the Flyers land Alexei Zhamnov from the Blackhawks in 2004 while Fraser was still playing junior with Red Deer in the WHL.

Being a British Columbia boy, Fraser played his minor hockey in the Vancouver area, at one time with teammates Troy Brouwer, Andrew Ladd, and Brent Seabrook, all currently with the Hawks. Incredibly, the three, along with Colin Fraser, also played for Canada at the 2005 World Junior Championship in Grand Forks, North Dakota, winning the gold medal.

After graduating from junior in 2005, Fraser played all of 2005-06 with Chicago's AHL affiliate in Norfolk, developing into a skilled and tough forward. He made his NHL debut the next year, but it wasn't until 2008-09 that he was with the Hawks full time.

Career Statistics		Regular Season					Playoffs				
		GP	G	A	P	Pim	GP	G	A	P	Pim
2006-07	CHI	1	0	0	0	2	DNQ				
2007-08	CHI	5	0	0	0	7	DNQ				
2008-09	CHI	81	6	11	17	55	2	0	0	0	2
2009-10	CHI	70	7	12	19	44	FOR 2010 PLAYOFF STATS SEE P. 28				
Totals		157	13	23	36	108					

FOR 2010 PLAYOFF STATS SEE P. 28

Hendry, Jordan

b. Lanigan, Saskatchewan, February 23, 1984

Defence—shoots left

6' 196 lbs.

Undrafted—signed as a free agent by Chicago on July 17, 2006

What Hendry lacks in raw talent he makes up for in other ways, notably skating and hitting. In truth, Hendry is the kind of player every team needs to win. He can play plenty of minutes in a game without being a liability, and his poise and tenacity are often more than the opposition can handle.

Hendry is another Hawks' success story, in that he played college hockey in Alaska for four years and was never drafted. Hard hitting and reliable with and without the puck, he worked his way into the Hawks' lineup through their AHL affiliate in Norfolk at the end of the 2005-06 season. Chicago liked what it saw and signed him to a two-year contract, and Hendry played much of the next two years with the Admirals, honing his skills at the professional level.

The Hawks were impressed by his impregnable defence, especially one-on-one, and his ability to kill penalties. They signed him to a two-year contract extension in 2008, meaning he'll be a free agent in the summer of 2010.

Career Statistics		Regular Season					Playoffs				
		GP	G	A	P	Pim	GP	G	A	P	Pim
2007-08	CHI	40	1	3	4	22	DNQ				
2008-09	CHI	9	0	0	0	4	DNP				
2009-10	CHI	43	2	6	8	10	FOR 2010 PLAYOFF STATS SEE P. 28				
Totals		92	3	9	12	36					

Hjalmarsson, Niklas

b. Eksjo, Sweden, June 6, 1987

Defence—shoots left

6'3" 205 lbs.

Drafted 108th overall by Chicago in 2005

Still only 23 years old, Hjalmarsson is the real deal in the eyes of Blackhawks' scouts and executives, and could turn into a Borje Salming-type player. He is talented with the puck and isn't afraid of a physical game without it, and after three years in the Swedish league he has improved every year since coming to North America.

Hjalmarsson split his first two pro seasons between the Hawks and the AHL affiliate in Rockford, where he matured and developed seemingly every game. He made the NHL full-time this past season and continued to improve. In 2009-10, he averaged some 20 minutes of ice time a game, a figure that increased during the more demanding playoffs of 2010.

The numbers don't yet show it, but the Hawks love Hjalmarsson's ability to move the puck and generate offense. He gets his fair share of power-play time as well, and coach Joel Quenneville quickly discovered the bigger the game, the bigger he plays. He isn't quite as well-known now as Toews, Kane, and Hossa, but make no mistake—an appropriate share of the team's success is because of Hajlmarsson's play from the blue line.

Career Statistics		Regular Season					Playoffs				
		GP	G	A	P	Pim	GP	G	A	P	Pim
2007-08	CHI	13	0	1	1	13	DNQ				
2008-09	CHI	21	1	2	3	0	17	0	1	1	6
2009-10	CHI	77	2	15	17	20	FOR 2010 PLAYOFF STATS SEE P. 28				
Totals		111	3	18	21	33					

Hossa, Marian

b. Stara Lubovna, Czechoslovakia
(Slovakia), January 12, 1979

Right wing—shoots left

6'1" 210 lbs.

Drafted 12th overall by Ottawa in 1997

The oddest thing about having Marian Hossa in the lineup for the Hawks in the 2010 playoffs was that he was with his third team—and in his third Stanley Cup Final—in as many years. But whereas he lost with Pittsburgh in 2008 and Detroit in 2009, he finally won an elusive Cup with the Hawks in 2010.

Even as a teen Hossa was a top prospect, and one of the few Europeans of his era to play junior hockey in Canada. Hossa played one season with Portland of the WHL, leading the Winter Hawks to the Memorial Cup in 1998. He also made his NHL debut with the Senators that year and the next fall he was in the NHL full time.

Hossa quickly became a bona fide star in the NHL, increasing his scoring from 15 to 29 to 32 goals in his first three seasons in Ottawa, and going to 45 two years after that. Although he was considered a major piece of the Stanley Cup puzzle with the Sens, his life was upended in the summer of 2005 when the team acquired Dany Heatley from Ottawa, sending Hossa to the Thrashers as part of the multi-player deal.

But Hossa continued to thrive in Georgia, registering 92 points his first year and 100 points (including 43 goals) in 2006-07. He was acquired by the Pittsburgh Penguins at the trade deadline in 2008, with Pittsburgh GM Ray Shero believing Sidney Crosby and Evgeni Malkin needed one more scorer to make the team a Cup contender. He was right. Hossa shone with the team, helping it to the Cup finals and scoring 12 goals in 20 playoff games along the way.

In the summer, though, Hossa rejected a huge contract offer from Pittsburgh, choosing to sign with Detroit for less money and what he perceived to be a better chance at the Cup, since the Red Wings had beaten the Pens for the Cup in '08. Hossa was wrong again. The reverse occurred in 2009 and he was on the losing end for a second straight year.

On July 1, 2009, Hossa decided to settle down. He signed a 12-year, $62.8-million contract with Chicago, one of the largest deals in league history, believing he could help the Hawks win the Cup several times over. Hossa missed the first two months recovering from off-season shoulder surgery, but he came back to continue his scoring ways.

Hossa's international resume is also impressive. He has represented Slovakia at the last three Olympics as well as at seven World Championships and two World Junior Championships.

Career Statistics		Regular Season					Playoffs				
		GP	G	A	P	Pim	GP	G	A	P	Pim
1997-98	OTT	7	0	1	1	0	DNP				
1998-99	OTT	60	15	15	30	37	4	0	2	2	4
1999-00	OTT	78	29	27	56	32	6	0	0	0	2
2000-01	OTT	81	32	43	75	44	4	1	1	2	4
2001-02	OTT	80	31	35	66	50	12	4	6	10	2
2002-03	OTT	80	45	35	80	34	18	5	11	16	6
2003-04	OTT	81	36	46	82	46	7	3	1	4	0
2005-06	ATL	80	39	53	92	67	DNQ				
2006-07	ATL	82	43	57	100	49	4	0	1	1	6
2007-08	ATL	60	26	30	56	30	--	--	--	--	--
2007-08	PIT	12	3	7	10	6	20	12	14	26	12
2008-09	DET	74	40	31	71	63	23	6	9	15	10
2009-10	CHI	57	24	27	51	18	FOR 2010 PLAYOFF STATS SEE P. 28				
Totals		832	363	407	770	476					

Huet, Cristobal

b. St. Martin d'Heres, France,
September 3, 1975

Goalie—catches left

6'1" 205 lbs.

Drafted 214th overall by Los Angeles in 2001

The number of players from France who have made the NHL is small, indeed, and the number of goalies can be counted on one finger. Cristobal Huet is the first. Huet wasn't even drafted until he was 25 years old, and it wasn't until two years later that he played his first NHL game, with Los Angeles. But he has learned to play on the smaller ice of North America and has developed his skills as a goalie to the point that he is now a bona fide big leaguer.

Before arriving in the NHL, Huet played for several years in the Swiss league, where he twice had the league's best goals-against average. As well, he played in the 1998 and 2002 Olympics for France. In the fall of 2002 he decided to give the NHL a chance, and the Kings assigned him to their AHL affiliate in Manchester. Huet was called up for a dozen games, recording a shutout to go with a very respectable GAA of 2.33.

Huet got a significant promotion when the Kings traded him to the Canadiens in 2004, but because of the lockout he returned to Europe and played in Germany for a year. The next season, 2005-06, he faced the pressure cooker that is Montreal, and being a Frenchman who played goal he was expected to follow in the footsteps of legends such as Vezina and Plante. He wasn't quite the hall of famer that these great men were, but he did win the starter's job from Jose Theodore, and for the better part of two years played the majority of games. Huet suffered a groin injury in early 2007, though, and missed almost two months trying to get back into game shape.

Midway through the 2007-08 season, however, the Habs sent him to Washington when it seemed Carey Price was going to be their superstar goalie, and in the summer of 2008 Huet signed with the Blackhawks as a free agent, the fourth stop of his NHL career. The four-year contract was worth $22.4 million, a clear indication of his role as a starter for the team.

Career Statistics		Regular Season						Playoffs					
		GP	W-L-T-O/T	Mins	GA	SO	GAA	GP	W-L	Mins	GA	SO	GAA
2002-03	LA	12	4-4-1-0	541	21	1	2.33	DNQ					
2003-04	LA	41	10-16-10-0	2,199	89	3	2.43	DNQ					
2005-06	MON	36	18-11-0-4	2,103	77	7	2.20	6	2-4	386	15	0	2.33
2006-07	MON	42	19-16-0-3	2,286	107	2	2.81	DNQ					
2007-08	MON	39	21-12-0-6	2,278	97	2	2.55	--	--	--	--	--	--
2007-08	WAS	13	11-2-0-0	771	21	2	1.63	7	3-4	451	22	0	2.93
2008-09	CHI	41	20-15-0-4	2,351	99	3	2.53	3	1-2	130	7	0	3.23
2009-10	CHI	48	26-14-0-4	2,731	114	4	2.50						
Totals		272	129-90-11-21	15,261	625	24	2.46						

FOR 2010 PLAYOFF STATS SEE P. 28

Kane, Patrick

b. Buffalo, New York, November 19, 1988

Right wing—shoots left

5'10" 178 lbs.

Drafted 1st overall by Chicago in 2007

One of the team's young studs, Patrick Kane has done nearly everything asked of him in his blossoming NHL career. He was the first overall draft choice in 2007 after an outstanding junior career on several fronts. For starters, he was part of the U.S. national team development program for two years (2004-06), the greenhouse program of USA Hockey designed to develop a small group of the nation's best teenagers.

Kane then went to the London Knights of the OHL for the 2006-07 season, where he led the OHL with 145 points and was named rookie of the year. He also played for USA at the 2007 World Junior Championship, winning a bronze medal. Indeed, he and current Chicago teammate Jonathan Toews faced each other in the memorable semi-finals shootout, won by Toews in the seventh round. Now 18, Kane headed to his first NHL training camp, made the Hawks, and never looked back.

As a rookie he led all scorers with 72 points and won the Calder Trophy, beating out Toews and Washington's Nicklas Backstrom. The Hawks didn't make the playoffs, and Kane appeared again for the United States internationally, this time at the 2008 World Championship.

Kane's goal production has increased every year he's been in the league, and playing on a line with Toews, the pair are the face of the team's bright and magical future. Toews is the set-up man for the scorer Kane, and this past season they were opponents at the 2010 Olympics. Kane had to settle for silver as his Americans lost 3-2 to Toews and Canada for Olympic gold, but given their youth and skill, it's likely this won't be either their last Stanley Cup win or their final international meeting.

Career Statistics		Regular Season					Playoffs				
		GP	G	A	P	Pim	GP	G	A	P	Pim
2007-08	CHI	82	21	51	72	52	DNQ				
2008-09	CHI	80	25	45	70	42	16	9	5	14	12
2009-10	CHI	82	30	58	88	20	FOR 2010 PLAYOFF STATS SEE P. 28				
Totals		244	76	154	230	114					

Keith, Duncan

b. Winnipeg, Manitoba, July 16, 1983

Defence—shoots left

6'1" 169 lbs.

Drafted 54th overall by Chicago in 2002

A peripatetic childhood has given way to NHL stability for Duncan Keith, who was born in Winnipeg, spent his early years in Fort Frances, Ontario, and then lived as a teen in Penticton, British Columbia. He moved to Michigan at age 18 to start a college career and continue along his path to the NHL.

Keith played in the historic "Cold War" outdoor game between Michigan and Michigan State (his alma mater), which set an attendance record for a hockey game at the start of the 2001-02 season. He played only a year and a half, however, before moving home and continuing his career in junior hockey with the Kelowna Rockets of the WHL, an increasingly common choice for young Canadian players.

Chicago drafted Keith in 2002, and after just half a season in the WHL the Hawks assigned him to their AHL farm team in Norfolk for the start of the 2003-04 season. He spent two full years away from the glare of the NHL, developing into a reliable defenceman with and without the puck. By 2005, he was ready to play a role with the Hawks, and he has responded with remarkable success.

Perhaps the two stats that best illustrate Keith's swift rise are his ice time and plus-minus rating. As a rookie, he led all Hawks' players with an average of more than 23 minutes a game, and this number has risen over the four years he has been with the team. At the same time, he was a -11 as a rookie, but in 2008-09 that number had risen sharply to a +33, when he was averaging a staggering 25:34 of ice time per game.

After his rookie season, the Hawks signed Keith to a five-year contract extension, but they had even bigger things in mind once they saw how great a player he was. In December 2009, they tore up this contract and drafted a new one which included 13 years and $72-million. Keith signed on the dotted line and, if all goes according to plan, the once travel-weary player will spend his entire career in one place—Chicago.

Keith was part of Canada's gold-medal team at the Vancouver Olympics in February 2010. His only previous international experience with Team Canada came at the 2008 World Championship in Quebec City, the 100th anniversary of the IIHF. The Hawks failed to make the playoffs that year, and Keith jumped at the opportunity to wear a maple leaf sweater. The team made it to the gold-medal game before losing to Russia 4-3 in overtime.

Career Statistics		Regular Season					Playoffs				
		GP	G	A	P	Pim	GP	G	A	P	Pim
2005-06	CHI	81	9	12	21	79	DNQ				
2006-07	CHI	82	2	29	31	76	DNQ				
2007-08	CHI	82	12	20	32	56	DNQ				
2008-09	CHI	77	8	36	44	60	17	0	6	6	10
2009-10	CHI	82	14	55	69	51	FOR 2010 PLAYOFF STATS SEE P. 28				
Totals		404	45	152	197	322					

FOR 2010 PLAYOFF STATS SEE P. 28

Kopecky, Tomas

b. Ilava, Czechoslovakia (Slovakia), February 5, 1982

Right Wing—shoots left

6'3" 203 lbs.

Drafted 38th overall by Detroit in 2000

A significant contributor to the Hawks' playoff success in 2010, Tomas Kopecky is the very model of how a European player can develop for the NHL, if he chooses to. He played junior as a teen in his home country of Slovakia, and after Detroit drafted him in 2000, he moved to Canada and played major junior in the WHL with Lethbridge for two years, during which time he saw some action in the AHL, the next level up.

During these formative years Kopecky was also active internationally for Slovakia. In 2000, he played at both the U18 and World Junior Championship, and in 2001 and '02 he again played at the World Juniors.

Kopecky then played for Grand Rapids for three solid years, never seeing the NHL and developing in an environment without pressure or expectations. In his fourth year with the Griffins, he got into one game with the Red Wings, and in 2006 he was on the team as a bona fide NHLer. That 2006-07 season, however, ended early for him thanks to a broken collarbone, but he recovered and was healthy the next year.

The Red Wings won the Stanley Cup that season, but after one more year in which he had only a limited role in the playoffs Kopecky decided to sign with Chicago. He made the right choice. The Red Wings were no longer a good fit, and the Hawks, like Kopecky himself, were young, with many years of promise ahead.

The 2009-10 season was a defining one for the centreman. He had a career best ten goals and represented Slovakia at the Olympics in Vancouver, and in the playoffs he thrived. Although he wasn't dressed for every game, he made the most of his chances, none bigger than Game One of the finals when he scored the game-winning goal. He was in the lineup only because Andrew Ladd was ill, but Kopecky turned a crazy 5-5 game after two periods into a win by getting the only goal of the third on a great move.

Career Statistics		Regular Season					Playoffs				
		GP	G	A	P	Pim	GP	G	A	P	Pim
2005-06	DET	1	0	0	0	2	DNP				
2006-07	DET	26	1	0	1	22	4	0	0	0	6
2007-08	DET	77	5	7	12	43	DNP				
2008-09	DET	79	6	13	19	46	8	0	1	1	7
2009-10	CHI	74	10	11	21	28	FOR 2010 PLAYOFF STATS SEE P. 28				
Totals		257	22	31	53	141					

Ladd, Andrew

b. Maple Ridge, British Columbia, December 12, 1985

Left wing—shoots left

6'2" 198 lbs.

Drafted 4th overall by Carolina in 2004

Before making his NHL debut as a 19-year-old, Ladd had a short but outstanding junior career in the WHL with the Calgary Hitmen. A power forward, he was drafted a lofty 4th overall by Carolina in 2004, and early in 2005 he was a member of Canada's gold-medal team at the World Junior Championship. That team also featured two current Hawks' teammates, Brent Seabrook and Colin Fraser.

Even more impressive, Ladd won the Stanley Cup with the Hurricanes in his rookie year, a frustrating season that ended happily. He started in Lowell but quickly moved up to the NHL, but after only a few games he suffered a knee injury and missed three months. When he was healthy, he was sent back to the AHL, but he played so well again that the 'Canes recalled him for the rest of the year. He was in the lineup for most of the playoffs during the team's run to its first Stanley Cup.

Ladd was traded to the Hawks for Tuomo Ruutu on February 26, 2008, and in his first full season with Chicago he had a career year with 49 points.

Career Statistics		Regular Season					Playoffs				
		GP	G	A	P	Pim	GP	G	A	P	Pim
2005-06	CAR	29	6	5	11	4	17	2	3	5	4
2006-07	CAR	65	11	10	21	46	DNQ				
2007-08	CAR	43	9	9	18	31	--	--	--	--	--
2007-08	CHI	20	5	7	12	4	DNQ				
2008-09	CHI	82	15	34	49	28	17	3	1	4	12
2009-10	CHI	82	17	21	38	67	FOR 2010 PLAYOFF STATS SEE P. 28				
Totals		321	63	86	149	180					

Madden, John

b. Toronto, Ontario, May 4, 1973

Centre—shoots left

5'11" 190 lbs.

Undrafted—signed as a free agent by New Jersey on June 26, 1997

The fact that John Madden has played nearly 800 regular-season games in the NHL and has won the Stanley Cup twice makes him the poster boy for perseverance. He grew up north of Toronto and played lower levels of junior hockey, never at the OHL or major level.

Madden was never drafted and was never a prototypical superstar. Although he did everything well, he didn't do one thing exceptionally, and as a result he flew under the radar for most of his four years with the University of Michigan. As luck would have it, New Jersey GM Lou Lamoriello was keeping close tabs on the Wolverines because of another player, Brendan Morrison, but every time he saw Morrison play he also took notice of Madden.

Lamoriello signed Madden to a contract in the summer of 1997, and the player spent most of the next two years with the farm team in Albany. His first full season in the NHL was 1999-2000. The Devils won the Stanley Cup, in part because of Madden's superior two-way play.

Indeed, Madden led the league in short-handed goals that year with six and was excellent on faceoffs and defensive play. The next year he won the Frank Selke Trophy, an honour for which he was nominated three more times in the next seven years.

Despite often playing against the other team's best stars, Madden also had some scoring ability. On six occasions he has had at least 15 goals in a year, and on October 29, 2000, he made history. He and teammate Randy McKay each scored four goals in a game, the first teammates to turn this trick since 1922.

A penalty killer and shot blocker, two-way player and leader, Madden was invaluable to the Devils for a decade. But in 2009, when he became an unrestricted free agent, he signed with the Hawks and brought his unique skill set to bear on another Cup triumph.

Career Statistics		Regular Season					Playoffs				
		GP	G	A	P	Pim	GP	G	A	P	Pim
1998-99	NJ	4	0	1	1	0	DNP				
1999-00	NJ	74	16	9	25	6	20	3	4	7	0
2000-01	NJ	80	23	15	38	12	25	4	3	7	6
2001-02	NJ	82	15	8	23	25	6	0	0	0	0
2002-03	NJ	80	19	22	41	26	24	6	10	16	2
2003-04	NJ	80	12	23	35	22	5	0	0	0	0
2005-06	NJ	82	16	20	36	36	9	4	1	5	8
2006-07	NJ	74	12	20	32	14	11	1	1	2	2
2007-08	NJ	80	20	23	43	26	5	2	1	3	2
2008-09	NJ	76	7	16	23	26	7	0	1	1	4
2009-10	NJ	79	10	13	23	12					
Totals		791	150	170	320	205					

FOR 2010 PLAYOFF STATS SEE P. 28

Niemi, Antti

b. Vantaa, Finland, August 29, 1983

Goalie—catches left

6'1" 200 lbs.

Undrafted—signed as a free agent by Chicago on May 5, 2008

It isn't very often a goalie will make his NHL debut at age 25, but Antti Niemi did just that on February 27, 2009. He played just one period, but two days later he made his first start and got his first win.

Niemi developed in his homeland of Finland, moving from second division to the top level in 2005 playing with the Pelicans of Lahti. The Hawks signed him as a free agent, and he spent most of 2008-09 with Rockford in the AHL, learning the North American game and adapting to the smaller sheet of NHL ice.

This 2009-10 season has been a special one for the goalie on three counts. First, he made the team during training camp. Second, he travelled with the Hawks to Finland where they and Florida Panthers began the NHL regular season. He sat on the bench for the first game, a 4-3 shootout loss, but he was the starter the next night and led Chicago to a 4-0 win, his first NHL shutout.

Niemi and Cristobal Huet more or less shared the goaltending duties during the 2009-10 regular season, but it was the Finn who took over as the main man in the playoffs. When he earned a shutout against Nashville in Game Two of the opening-round series, he became the first Chicago goalie to do so since Ed Belfour in 1996. Four nights later, he got a second shutout, the first netminder to earn two blank sheets for the team since Tony Esposito in 1974.

Career Statistics		Regular Season						Playoffs					
		GP	W-L-T-O/T	Mins	GA	SO	GAA	GP	W-L	Mins	GA	SO	GAA
2008-09	CHI	3	1-1-0-1	141	8	0	3.40	DNP					
2009-10	CHI	39	26-7-0-4	2,190	82	7	2.25	FOR 2010 PLAYOFF STATS SEE P. 28					
Totals		42	27-8-0-5	2,332	90	7	2.32						

Seabrook, Brent

b. Richmond, British Columbia, April 20, 1985

Defence—shoots right

6'3" 218 lbs.

Drafted 14th overall by Chicago in 2003

Brent Seabrook played minor hockey with the Pacific Vipers in Tsawwassen, British Columbia, where three other future Chicago Blackhawks' teammates also played—Andrew Ladd, Troy Brouwer, and Colin Fraser. Seabrook was drafted by the Hawks 14th overall in 2003, after leading Canada to a gold medal at the World U18 Championship.

Although the defenceman was still two years away from joining the NHL, he made the most of his major junior career with Lethbridge, as well as with Team Canada at the World Junior Championship, winning a silver and gold medal in successive seasons.

Seabrook made the Hawks at training camp in 2005 and has been a mainstay on the blue line ever since, averaging more than 20 minutes a game throughout his career. One of the more unsung players on Canada's 2010 Olympic team, he had partnered so effectively with Duncan Keith in Chicago that executive director Steve Yzerman decided to name both players to the Olympic team for Vancouver. The pair complemented each other perfectly and, given their experience as a tandem, it only made sense to bring them to a short tournament such as the Olympics where communication and cohesion are major factors for success.

Winning gold with Canada at the 2010 Olympics added a final level of accomplishment to the Seabrook resume, as he has now played for Canada at every major IIHF tournament: U18, the World Juniors, the World Championship, and the Olympics. Although he is blessed with some ability in the offensive zone, he is known more for his superb work inside his own blue line, limiting scoring chances and moving the puck up ice quickly and effectively.

Career Statistics		Regular Season					Playoffs				
		GP	G	A	P	Pim	GP	G	A	P	Pim
2005-06	CHI	69	5	27	32	60	DNQ				
2006-07	CHI	81	4	20	24	104	DNQ				
2007-08	CHI	82	9	23	32	90	DNQ				
2008-09	CHI	82	8	18	26	62	17	1	11	12	14
2009-10	CHI	78	4	26	30	59	FOR 2010 PLAYOFF STATS SEE P. 28				
Totals		392	30	114	144	375					

Sharp, Patrick

b. Winnipeg, Manitoba, December 27, 1981

Centre—shoots right

6'1" 199 lbs.

Drafted 95th overall by Philadelphia in 1997

One of a group of current Hawks who started his career with the team's Cup-finalist opponents Philadelphia, Sharp has turned into a valuable player with plenty of offensive skill and defensive commitment. He went to the University of Vermont for two years (2000-02) during which time he was drafted by the Flyers. In 2002, he left college to start a pro career that has developed impressively ever since.

In his first year, Sharp played mostly in the AHL. In his second year, he split the season between the Flyers and Phantoms. His third year was all in the AHL because of the lockout, and at training camp in 2005 he was mature and ready for the NHL. However, after just 22 games the Flyers traded him to Chicago in what looked like a minor deal. He and Eric Meloche headed to the Blackhawks and the Flyers got a 3rd-round draft choice in 2006.

The Hawks won the deal by a wide margin because they got the best player. Sharp scored 20 goals in his first full season with Chicago and 36 the next year—superstar numbers. He has tapered off the last couple of seasons, but this past year he was also a +24 in the plus/minus stat, an impressive number for a scoring forward. He also had a career-high 66 points.

As a result of his 36-goal season, and the Hawks missing the playoffs, Sharp was invited to play for Team Canada at the 2008 World Championship in Quebec City and Halifax, the 100th anniversary of the IIHF and first time the tournament was played in Canada. He helped the team win a silver medal, and the event further developed his skills as he played against the best players from around the world.

Career Statistics		Regular Season					Playoffs				
		GP	G	A	P	Pim	GP	G	A	P	Pim
2002-03	PHI	3	0	0	0	2	DNP				
2003-04	PHI	41	5	2	7	55	12	1	0	1	2
2005-06	PHI	22	5	3	8	10	--	--	--	--	--
2005-06	CHI	50	9	14	23	36	DNQ				
2006-07	CHI	80	20	15	35	74	DNQ				
2007-08	CHI	80	36	26	62	55	DNQ				
2008-09	CHI	61	26	18	44	41	17	7	4	11	6
2009-10	CHI	82	25	41	66	28	FOR 2010 PLAYOFF STATS SEE P. 28				
Totals		419	126	119	245	301					

FOR 2010 PLAYOFF STATS SEE P. 28

Sopel, Brent

b. Calgary, Alberta, January 7, 1977

Defence—shoots right

6'1" 201 lbs.

Drafted 144th overall by Vancouver in 1995

One of the veterans on a young Hawks team at age 33, Sopel is a skilled, stay-at-home defenceman who gives his team plenty of minutes, often playing in key situations. He developed slowly but consistently in the Vancouver system, moving progressively from junior in Swift Current to the AHL with Syracuse and finally to the Canucks. In all, it was seven years before he established himself as a bona fide NHL defenceman, but once he had done so there was no looking back.

Sopel's career can be broken down into three distinct eras. First, his early years with the Canucks, which lasted until the lockout season of 2004-05. Then came two years of transitory play. Vancouver traded him to the New York Islanders and less than a year later he was on the move to Los Angeles and back to Vancouver.

When his contract expired in 2007, he went to training camp with Detroit but was given a superior contract offer from Chicago. He signed with the Blackhawks, and it was then the third part of his career began. He had a terrific season in 2007-08, and midway through that year the Hawks extended his contract through to 2011. The next year ended after only 23 games, however, because of a serious elbow injury that required season-ending rehabilitation.

Healthy again for 2009-10, Sopel has been a vital part of the team's march to the Stanley Cup.

Career Statistics		Regular Season					Playoffs				
		GP	G	A	P	Pim	GP	G	A	P	Pim
1998-99	VAN	5	1	0	1	4	DNQ				
1999-00	VAN	18	2	4	6	12	DNQ				
2000-01	VAN	52	4	10	14	10	4	0	0	0	2
2001-02	VAN	66	8	17	25	44	6	0	2	2	2
2002-03	VAN	81	7	30	37	23	14	2	6	8	4
2003-04	VAN	80	10	32	42	36	7	0	1	1	0
2005-06	NYI	57	2	25	27	64	--	--	--	--	--
2005-06	LA	11	0	1	1	6	DNQ				
2006-07	LA	44	4	19	23	14	--	--	--	--	--
2006-07	VAN	20	1	4	5	10	11	0	0	0	2
2007-08	CHI	58	1	19	20	28	DNQ				
2008-09	CHI	23	1	1	2	8	DNP				
2009-10	CHI	73	1	7	8	34	FOR 2010 PLAYOFF STATS SEE P. 28				
Totals		588	42	169	211	293					

FOR 2010 PLAYOFF STATS SEE P. 28

Toews, Jonathan

b. Winnipeg, Manitoba, April 29, 1988

Centre—shoots left

6'2" 210 lbs.

Drafted 3rd overall by Chicago in 2006

Toews is the newest member of the Triple Gold Club. He won World Championship gold with Canada in 2007 and Olympic gold in February in Vancouver. This Stanley Cup win makes him the youngest of 25 people to have won the three great championships (24 players and one coach).

Although Toews won gold with Canada's juniors in 2006, he was a 17-year-old who was there more for the experience than as a player Team Canada was counting on. Not so the next year when he had one of the most memorable games in World Junior Championship history. In the semi-finals, Canada faced arch-rivals the United States, and after 60 minutes of regulation and ten minutes of overtime, the game was still tied.

Toews beat goalie Jeffrey Frazee during the opening round of the shootout, but this was tied 2–2, so sudden death shots were needed. Coach Craig Hartsburg returned to Toews after one failed round, and Toews scored again. So did the Americans. Another scoreless round had Hartsburg calling Toews's name for a third time, and for a third time Toews scored. This time, Carey Price

made one final save, and Canada went on to win the gold medal, all thanks to Toews's record three shootout goals in one game.

Later that season, he became one of a rare group of players to represent Canada at the World Championship without having NHL experience, and he completed an even rarer double by becoming the first Canadian to win gold at the World Junior and Senior Championships in the same season.

That anecdote points to the poise and maturity of the young player who had been drafted 3rd overall the previous year by Chicago. Toews finished his second year at North Dakota and then joined the Hawks as a rookie for the 2007–08 season at age 20. On October 10, 2007, Toews scored a goal on his first shot in his first NHL game and went on to record points in his first ten NHL games, the second-longest such streak in league history.

After a rookie season in which he scored 24 goals and 54 points in just 64 games, Toews was runner-up to teammate Patrick Kane in Calder Trophy voting (Kane played all 82 games and had 72 points). That summer, at age 20, Toews was named team captain of the Hawks, the third youngest in league history after Vincent Lecavalier and Sidney Crosby. In his second season on a rebuilding Chicago team, Toews had 34 goals and took the Hawks to the Conference Final in the playoffs before losing to Detroit in five games.

Career Statistics		Regular Season						Playoffs				
		GP	G	A	P	Pim		GP	G	A	P	Pim
2007-08	CHI	62	24	30	54	44		DNQ				
2008-09	CHI	82	34	35	69	51		17	7	6	13	26
2009-10	CHI	76	25	43	68	47		FOR 2010 PLAYOFF STATS SEE P. 28				
Totals		220	83	108	191	142						

Versteeg, Kris

b. Lethbridge, Alberta, May 13, 1986

Left wing—shoots right

5'10" 182 lbs.

Drafted 134th overall by Boston in 2004

One of the team's superstars-in-the-making, Versteeg signed a three-year contract extension with the Hawks in the summer of 2009 for $9 million, the result of an excellent rookie season.

Versteeg started his NHL career with the Boston Bruins organization when they drafted him in 2004, but did not see any ice time with the club. Indeed, Versteeg played under the radar for his four years in the WHL, primarily with Lethbridge, and on February 3, 2007, the prospect was traded to Chicago with future considerations for Brandon Bochenski.

Versteeg made his NHL debut, with the Hawks, on November 22, 2007, but spent most of the season with Norfolk in the AHL. When he came to camp a year later—bigger, stronger, more experienced—he made the team right away and promptly scored 22 goals as a rookie. He replicated his performance this past year, but in the playoffs coach Joel Quenneville asked him to change roles and he excelled.

As the 2010 playoffs moved along, Versteeg was taken off the second line and put on the third line with Andrew Ladd and Dave Bolland, essentially going from scorer to checker. The move paid off as Versteeg filed his ego and played for the team, doing sensational work as a checker. His offence declined, but the team thrived.

Career Statistics		Regular Season					Playoffs				
		GP	G	A	P	Pim	GP	G	A	P	Pim
2007-08	CHI	13	2	2	4	6	DNQ				
2008-09	CHI	78	22	31	53	55	17	4	8	12	22
2009-10	CHI	79	20	24	44	35	for 2010 playoff stats see p. 28				
Totals		170	44	57	101	96					

for 2010 playoff stats see p. 28

Acknowledgements

The author would like to thank the various people who have made this book possible. First to publisher Jordan Fenn for (as ever) continued support and enthusiasm for the great game on ice. To his assistant Sheila Douglas for helping everything move along as it should. To designers Michael Gray and Rob Scanlan at First Image, still the best place around to produce instant books instantly while maintaining the highest standards of design and production. To Fred Cheatham at Friesen's for printing the book at lightning speed without any loss of quality, and to Getty Images for supplying all of the photography—Paul Michinard, Wilfred Tenaillon, Cynthia Edorh, Jason Sundberg, Bruce Bennett, and Glenn Levy. And lastly to my family for support off the ice—Liz, Ian, Zac, Emily, me mom, and, of course, me frau, Mary Jane, without whom things just wouldn't be nearly as much fun.

Photo Credits